Internet Marketing FAST

Become a Thrive Expert

Internet Marketing Fast

Become a Thrive Expert

Copyright and Enquiries

Comments or enquiries may be left in the *Contact Me* page at:

https://superaffiliatechallenge.com/contact-me/

Internet Marketing Fast

Become a Thrive Expert

Contents

Copyright and Enquiries 2

The Essential Thrive 10

Thrive Plugins 10

    Thrive Leads 11

    Thrive Quiz Builder 11

    Thrive Ultimatum 11

    Thrive Ovation 11

    Clever Widgets 11

    Headline Optimizer 11

    Thrive Apprentice 11

    Thrive Comments 11

    Thrive Optimize 11

Thrive Leads 11

    Lead Groups 14

    Opt-in Forms 16

    Lightbox 17

        Edit the Form's Design 19

    Choose When the Form Appears 21

        Exit Intent 23

    Choose How Often the Form Appears 24

    Choose How the Form Appears 25

Internet Marketing Fast

Become a Thrive Expert

See Your Form in Action 27

Choose Where Your Form Appears 27

Save Your Choice as a Template 30

Lead Shortcodes.. 30

    Edit the Form's Design 34

ThriveBoxes 37

Signup Segue 41

Thrive Quiz Builder 48

Thrive Ultimatum 59

Thrive Ovation... 69

Clever Widgets 79

Headline Optimizer 82

Thrive Apprentice.. 89

    Lessons, Chapters and Modules 97

Thrive Comments... 98

Thrive Optimize.. 102

The Rest of the Books 109

Available Now 109

Not Yet Available.. 109

About the Author 111

Internet Marketing Fast

Become a Thrive Expert

Table of Figures

Figure 1: Thrive Leads Dashboard.................................... 12

Figure 2: Thrive Leads Menu Item 13

Figure 3: Add a New Lead Group 15

Figure 4: Give the Lead Group a Name............................ 15

Figure 5: Add an Opt-in Form 16

Figure 6: Select Opt-in Form to Create 16

Figure 7: Add a Lightbox Form 17

Figure 8: Start the Form Creation 18

Figure 9: Give the Lightbox Form a Name 19

Figure 10: The New Lightbox Form is Listed 19

Figure 11: Select a Template for Your Lightbox............... 20

Figure 12: Modify the Selected Template 21

Figure 13: Default Appearance Trigger............................ 22

Figure 14: Select Trigger Setting 22

Figure 15: Exit Intent Trigger 23

Figure 16: Choose the Display Frequency........................ 24

Figure 17: Select the Number of Days to Wait 24

Figure 18: Determine How the Form Appears.................. 25

Figure 19: Select the Desired Animation 26

Figure 20: The Form Is Listed Under the Lead Group 27

Figure 21: Choose Device(s).. 27

Figure 22: Select Your Targeting Options 28

Figure 23: Specify Where the Form is to Appear.............. 28

Figure 24: Basic Settings for Form Appearance 29

Figure 25: Select Individual Pages for Form Display 30

Figure 26: Save the Parameters as a Template 30

Figure 27: Add a New Lead Shortcode............................. 31

Figure 28: Give the Lead Shortcode a Name 32

Internet Marketing Fast

Become a Thrive Expert

Figure 29: New Lead Shortcode Created 32
Figure 30: Click Edit to Start the Form Design 33
Figure 31: Click the Create Form Button 33
Figure 32: Give the Lead Shortcode Form a Name 34
Figure 33: The New Lead Shortcode Form is Listed......... 34
Figure 34: Select a Template for Your Form 35
Figure 35: The Selected Template Can Be Modified........ 36
Figure 36: Add the Lead Shortcode to a Page.................. 37
Figure 37: The Lead Shortcode Form is Shown................ 37
Figure 38: Add a New ThriveBox....................................... 38
Figure 39: Give the ThriveBox a Name 38
Figure 40: Edit the ThriveBox... 39
Figure 41: Click the Create ThriveBox Form Button 39
Figure 42: Give the New Form a Name............................. 40
Figure 43: Edit the New Form's Design............................ 40
Figure 44: Choose a ThriveBox Template 41
Figure 45: Copy the ThriveBox Shortcode 41
Figure 46: Add New Signup Seque.................................... 43
Figure 47: Click the Add Signup Segue Button................. 43
Figure 48: Click No Connections Set 44
Figure 49: Select Your Webinar Platform 44
Figure 50: Choose Your Mailing List and Group 45
Figure 51: Select Your Redirect Destination 46
Figure 52: Select the Type of Redirect............................. 46
Figure 53: Select Signup Segue Thank You Page 47
Figure 54: Copy the Link... 47
Figure 55: The Link Generated by Signup Segue 48
Figure 56: Replace the Name and Email Tokens 48
Figure 57: Select Quiz Builder in Thrive Product Manager49

Internet Marketing Fast

Become a Thrive Expert

Figure 58: Select the Quiz Builder Dashboard 50

Figure 59: Click the + Button to Create a New Quiz 51

Figure 60: Select a Quiz Template 52

Figure 61: Give Your Quiz a Name 52

Figure 62: Choose Your Quiz Type 53

Figure 63: Add the Categories 54

Figure 64: Choose a Quiz Style................................... 55

Figure 65: Edit the Results Page 55

Figure 66: Quiz Flow... 56

Figure 67: Select Question Type 57

Figure 68: Enter Question and Answers 58

Figure 69: Install Thrive Ultimatum 59

Figure 70: Load the Ultimatum Dashboard 60

Figure 71: Choose Your Campaign Type 61

Figure 72: Name Your Ultimatum Campaign 62

Figure 73: Select a Display Mode................................. 62

Figure 74: Choose Where the Campaign is Displayed 63

Figure 75: Select the Lockdown Options 64

Figure 76: Design the Look of Your Countdown Timer..... 65

Figure 77: Modify the Ribbon Using Thrive Architect 65

Figure 78: Change the Design for the Last 3 Days 66

Figure 79: Showing the Campaign's Timeline 67

Figure 80: Start the Ultimatum Campaign 68

Figure 81: The Campaign Has Started............................ 69

Figure 82: Click to Access Thrive Ovation 70

Figure 83: Capture Testimonials with Architect 71

Figure 84: The Capture Testimonials Element................. 72

Figure 85: Choose a Capture Testimonial Template......... 72

Figure 86: Basic Page from Ovation Template................. 73

Internet Marketing Fast

Become a Thrive Expert

Figure 87: Click the Form Settings Button 74

Figure 88: Edit the Ovation Form's Fields 75

Figure 89: Set Testimonial Ready for Display 76

Figure 90: Select the Display Testimonials Element 77

Figure 91: Select a Display Template 78

Figure 92: Testimonial Display 79

Figure 93: Install Clever Widgets 80

Figure 94: Select Widgets 80

Figure 95: Select Thrive Widget Display Options............. 81

Figure 96: Control When Widget is Displayed 81

Figure 97: Install Headline Optimizer 82

Figure 98: Load Thrive Headline Optimizer 83

Figure 99: Click the Add New Button............................. 84

Figure 100: Choose Posts or Pages to Test 85

Figure 101: Content to be Tested 86

Figure 102: Create Your Variations............................... 87

Figure 103: Setting Test Criteria 88

Figure 104: Optimizer Test Summary 89

Figure 105: Install Thrive Apprentice............................ 90

Figure 106: Click Apprentice Dashboard........................ 91

Figure 107: Select or Create Your Training Page 92

Figure 108: Set up the Course Template 92

Figure 109: Click Add New Course 94

Figure 110: Enter the Course Name and Description 95

Figure 111: Course Has Been Created 95

Figure 112: Access Restrictions.................................... 97

Figure 113: Lesson YouTube Options............................. 98

Figure 114: Install Thrive Comments 99

Figure 115: Thrive Comments Dashboard 100

Internet Marketing Fast

Become a Thrive Expert

Figure 116: Set up Voting and Badges 101

Figure 117: Install Thrive Optimize 102

Figure 118: Click on A/B Test 103

Figure 119: Add the Page Variation 103

Figure 120: Duplicate Control Page 104

Figure 121: Two Variations Created 105

Figure 122: Set up the A/B Test 105

Figure 123: Personalize Your Test.................................. 106

Figure 124: Set the Goal and Start the Test.................. 106

Figure 125: Thrive Optimize Dashboard 107

Internet Marketing Fast

Become a Thrive Expert

The Essential Thrive

Book 6 in the Internet Marketing FAST series, *Building Your Website with Thrive*, covered getting Thrive Themes and Plugins, installing the Product Manager plugin, installing a theme and some essential plugins, customizing your WordPress website and the basic use of Thrive Architect, Thrive's drag and drop page editor.

Book 7 in the Internet Marketing FAST series, *Continue Your Journey with Thrive*, covered the remaining elements in the Thrive Architect plugin.

This user guide covers the rest of the Thrive plugins, along with some additional recommended plugins for such things as website backup and restore, connectivity to Google Analytics and so on.

To purchase Thrive Themes or simply to investigate further, please click:

THRIVE THEMES AND PLUGINS

Thrive Plugins

Here is a list of the remaining 9 Thrive plugins. Each is a link. You can click on any one of them to go to its explanation.

Internet Marketing Fast

Become a Thrive Expert

Thrive Leads

Thrive Quiz Builder

Thrive Ultimatum

Thrive Ovation

Clever Widgets

Headline Optimizer

Thrive Apprentice

Thrive Comments

Thrive Optimize

Thrive Leads

If all you want to do is put an in-line form on your post or page to collect a name and email address for your mailing list, the simplest solution is to use Thrive Architect's Lead Generation element. This is covered in Book 7 in the Internet Marketing FAST series, *Continue Your Journey with Thrive*.

Thrive Leads is different. With Thrive Leads, you can build one or more richly formatted opt-ins and then control when and how they appear. For example, you might create a

Internet Marketing Fast

Become a Thrive Expert

"Wait, don't go…" opt-in as a light box and then make it appear when the visitor is about to leave your site.

After you've installed the plugin, the Thrive Leads dashboard appears under the Thrive Dashboard.

Thrive Leads

Create and manage opt-in forms, keep track of your email list building and more.

THRIVE LEADS DASHBOARD

Figure 1: Thrive Leads Dashboard

or you can just click on the Thrive Leads menu item.

Internet Marketing Fast

Become a Thrive Expert

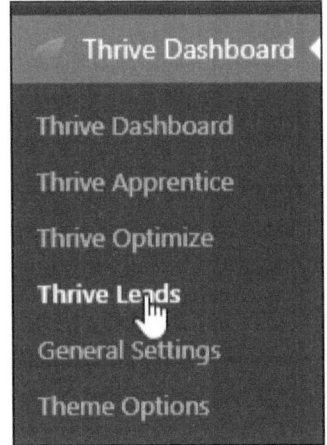

Figure 2: Thrive Leads Menu Item

With Thrive Leads, you can build 10 different types of opt-in forms:

1. <u>ThriveBox (Pop-Up Lightbox)</u>. An unblockable overlay (a.k.a. popup) that is displayed above your content and is very attention-grabbing.
2. <u>Sticky Ribbon</u>. Add a ribbon type form which shows at the top of the screen and remains "sticky" as the visitor scrolls down the page.
3. <u>Inline Forms</u>. Automatically insert an opt-in form at the bottom of your posts or insert them anywhere using a simple short code.
4. <u>2-Step Opt-In Forms</u>. Create a 2-step signup process by adding buttons or links that open a lightbox on click.
5. <u>Slide-In</u>. Less intrusive than a popup, but almost equally attention grabbing, this form slides into view from the corner.

6. <u>Opt-In Widget</u>. Add an opt-in form to your sidebar or any other widget area on your site, with just a few clicks.
7. <u>Screen Filler Overlay</u>. The "unignorable" opt-in form and the perfect way to make sure you get your visitor's full attention on your offer.
8. <u>Content Lock</u>. A great way to add an opt-in incentive right inside your content. Reveal it once the visitor signs up!
9. <u>Scroll Mat</u>. A unique type of screen-filling offer that appears from the top of the page and pushes the content down.
10. <u>Yes/No and Multiple-Choice Forms</u>. Engage your visitors and boost conversion rates by offering multiple choices!

It's important to understand that Thrive Leads are not built into a particular page or post.

They are created independently and then additional parameters are entered to specify what pages and posts they will appear on, what they will look like and how and when they will appear.

There is a hierarchy to Thrive Leads.

First, a Lead Group is specified. It normally relates to a specific promotion and it contains one or more Forms. The Form determines the appearance and the Lead Group determines when, where and how the Form will appear.

Lead Groups

Click the **Add New** button to create a new Lead Group.

Internet Marketing Fast

Become a Thrive Expert

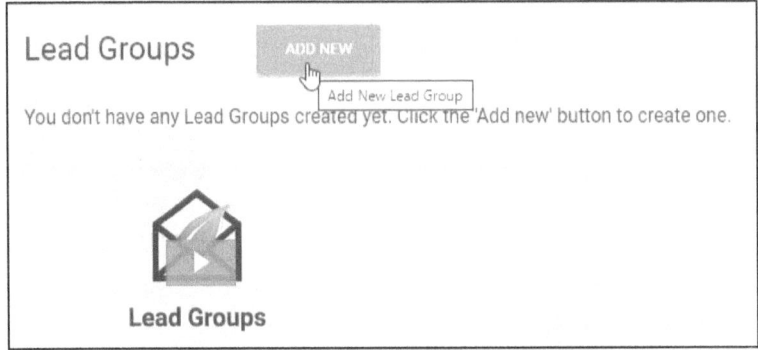

Figure 3: Add a New Lead Group

Give the new Lead Group a name that reflects your promotion.

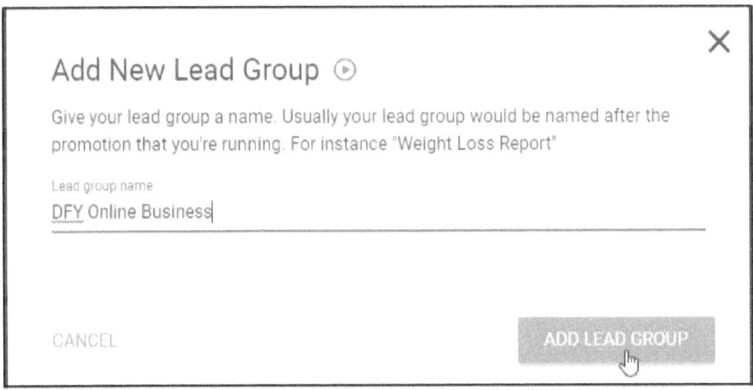

Figure 4: Give the Lead Group a Name

Then click the **ADD LEAD GROUP** button.

Once you've created your Lead Group, you can add different types of opt-in forms to it and control when and how they appear.

Internet Marketing Fast

Become a Thrive Expert

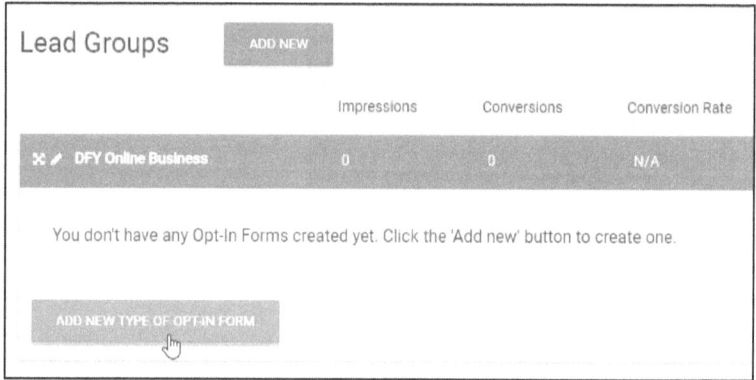

Figure 5: Add an Opt-in Form

Opt-in Forms

Click the **ADD NEW TYPE OF OPT-IN FORM** button. Then select from nine different types:

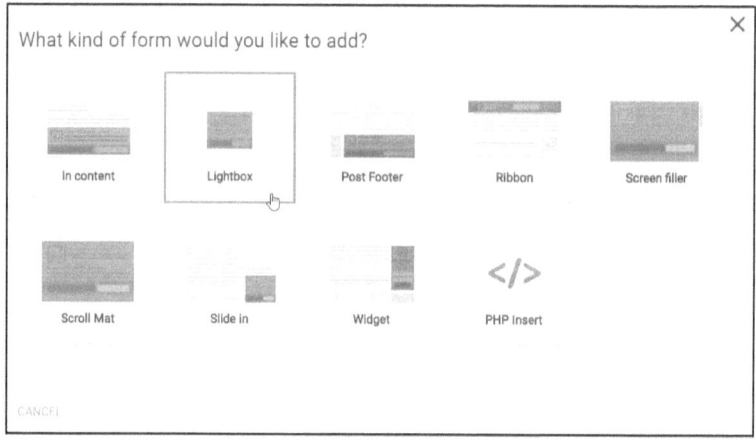

Figure 6: Select Opt-in Form to Create

You can work through each of these to become familiar with all of them.

Internet Marketing Fast

Become a Thrive Expert

Lightbox

As an example, we'll have a look at one of the most popular, the Lightbox.

Select Lightbox then proceed to the next step, adding a lightbox form.

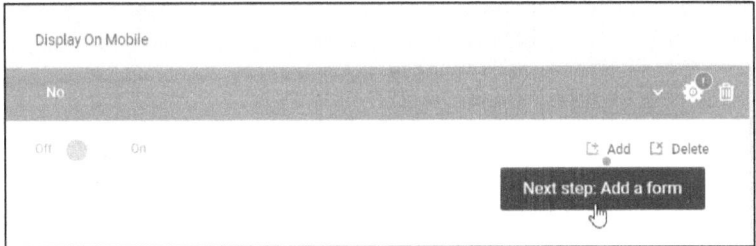

Figure 7: Add a Lightbox Form

Then start the form creation.

Internet Marketing Fast

Become a Thrive Expert

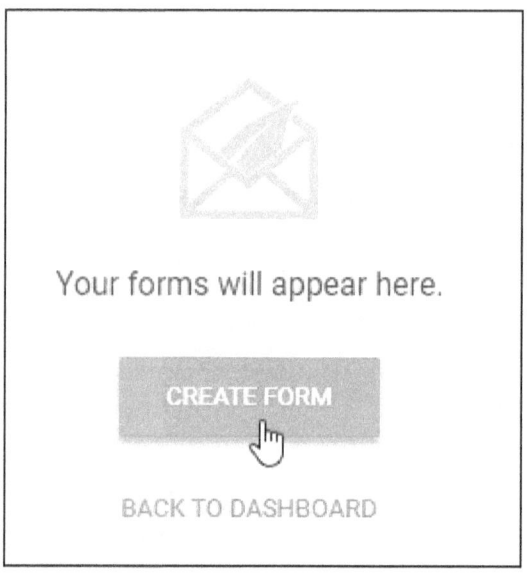

Figure 8: Start the Form Creation

Click the **CREATE FORM** button.

Give your new form a name. Note that it already appears in the Lead Group *DFY Online Business* as a *Lightbox*, so there is no point in repeating these. One approach is to call it something like *Variation 1*, as you may wish to try other alternative appearances further down the track.

Internet Marketing Fast

Become a Thrive Expert

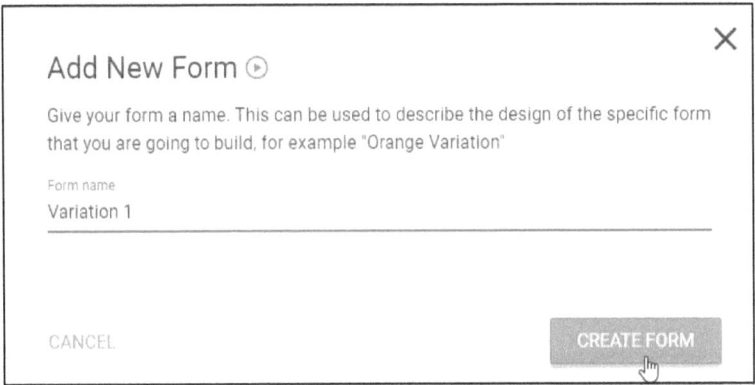

Figure 9: Give the Lightbox Form a Name

The new lightbox form will be listed under the Lead Group, and you can proceed to edit its design. You can also control other aspects of the form, such as when it appears and also add more forms.

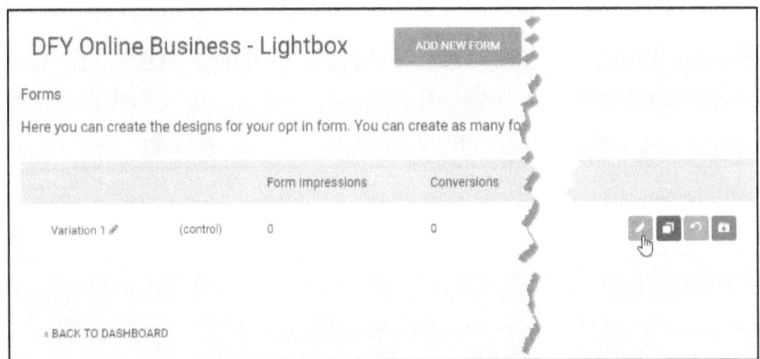

Figure 10: The New Lightbox Form is Listed

Edit the Form's Design

Click on the **Edit Design** icon as shown above. This will load Thrive Architect for you to design the form.

Internet Marketing Fast

Become a Thrive Expert

Start by selecting a template to use.

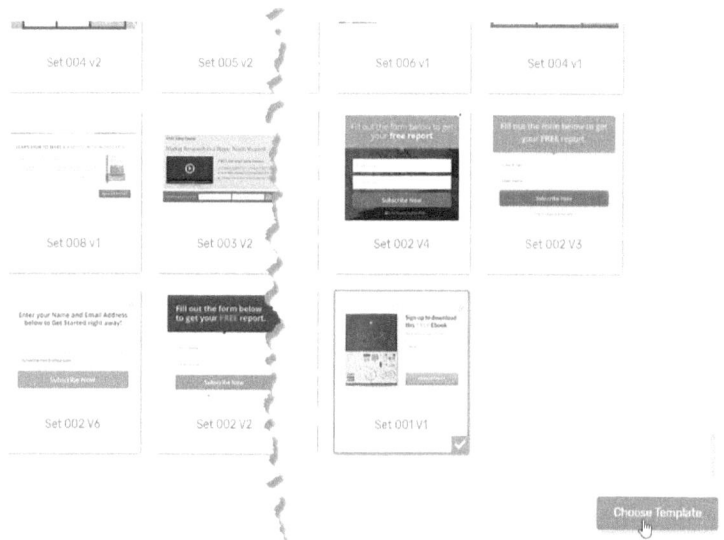

Figure 11: Select a Template for Your Lightbox

Note that there are a lot of templates. Scroll down to see them all. Select one by clicking on it and then click the **Choose Template** button.

Internet Marketing Fast

Become a Thrive Expert

Figure 12: Modify the Selected Template

Using Thrive Architect, the selected template can be modified to suit your purposes.

At the very least with the above template, you would change the image to the book you are giving away and modify the Lead Generation element to connect to your autoresponder.

Note that the process of connecting a Lead Gen element to your autoresponder is covered in *Book 6: Building Your Website.*

Choose When the Form Appears

By default, the lightbox is triggered as soon as a page is displayed, but this can be changed.

Internet Marketing Fast

Become a Thrive Expert

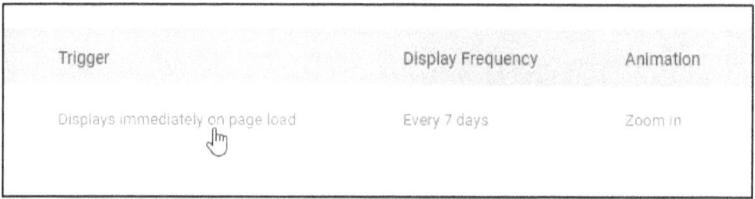

Figure 13: Default Appearance Trigger

You can change when the light box appears, by selecting from:

- Show on page load (the default)
- Show after a certain period of time
- Show when the user scrolls to a specific part of the content
- Show when the user clicks an element
- Show when the user is about to exit the page (exit intent)
- Show when the user reaches the bottom of the page

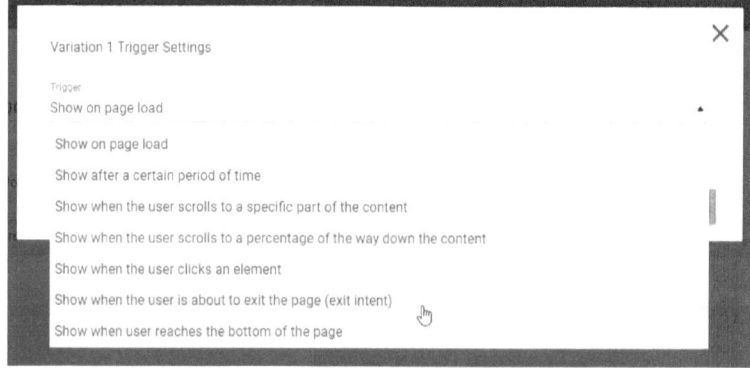

Figure 14: Select Trigger Setting

Note that the actual pages that the form will be shown on have not yet been determined. This is set at the Lead Group level and is covered further down.

Exit Intent

Exit intent is one of the most useful triggers, as it allows you to bring a new offer to the visitor just as they are about to leave, but doesn't apply to mobile devices, so typically you would use a delayed display in that case.

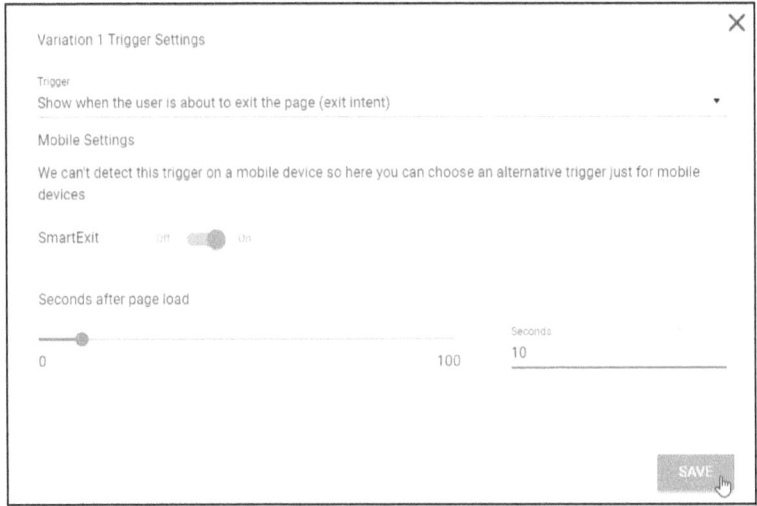

Figure 15: Exit Intent Trigger

Internet Marketing Fast

Become a Thrive Expert

Choose How Often the Form Appears

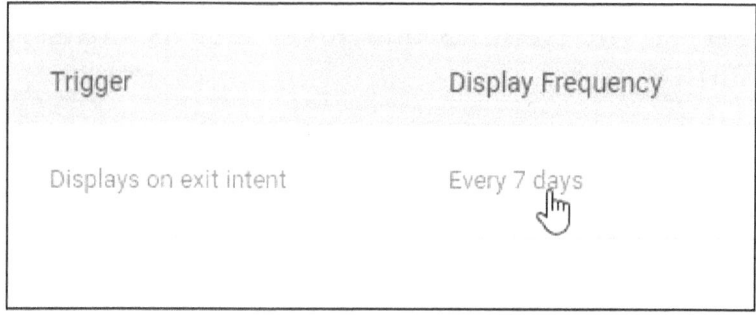

Figure 16: Choose the Display Frequency

To avoid annoying a visitor by presenting the same pop-up every time they visit, you can change how often the form appears to the same visitor.

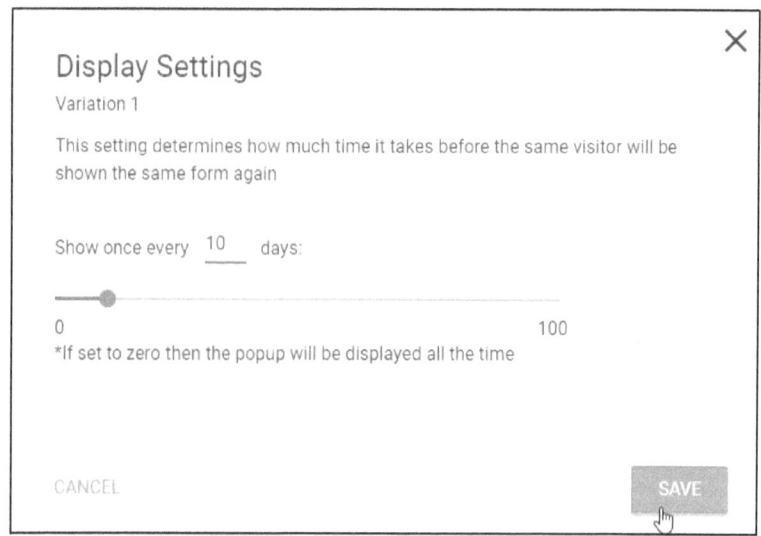

Figure 17: Select the Number of Days to Wait

Change the number of days to wait by entering it directly or moving the slider.

Choose How the Form Appears

Trigger	Display Frequency	Animation
Displays on exit intent	Every 10 days	Zoom In

Figure 18: Determine How the Form Appears

The form can make its appearance on screen in a number of different ways. Choose from

- Zoom In (the default)
- Instant
- Zoom Out
- Rotational
- Slide in from top
- Slide in from Bottom
- Slide in from Left
- Slide in from Right
- 3D Slit
- 3D Flip (Horizontal)
- 3D Flip (Vertical)
- 3D Sign
- 3D Rotate Bottom
- 3D Rotate Left
- Blur

- Make Way
- Slip from Top
- Bounce In
- Bounce In Down
- Bounce In Left
- Bounce In Right
- Bounce In Up

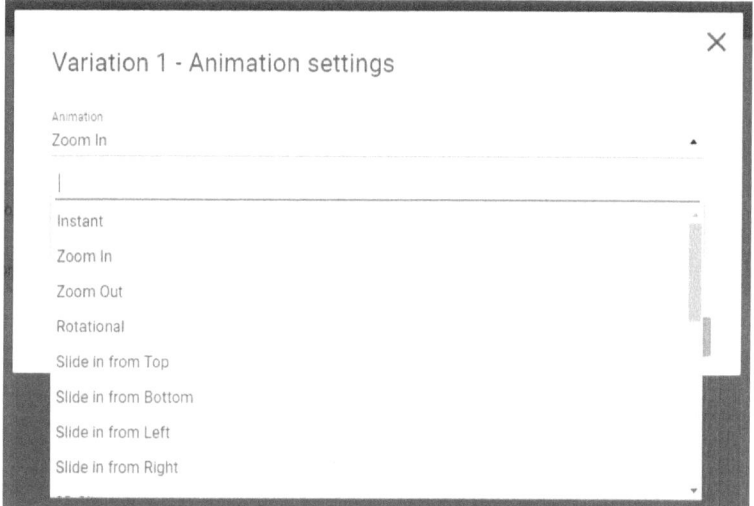

Figure 19: Select the Desired Animation

From here, you can add another form, modify any aspect of the form you have just created or return to the Lead Group that the form is part of.

If you return to the Lead Group, you will see your new form listed there.

Internet Marketing Fast

Become a Thrive Expert

See Your Form in Action

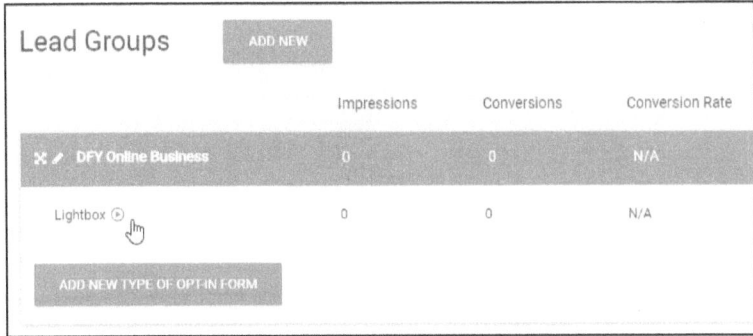

Figure 20: The Form Is Listed Under the Lead Group

Click on the little arrow next to the form to see exactly how it will appear on your website, including the animation.

Choose Where Your Form Appears

First, select whether your form is to appear on desktop computers, mobile devices or both.

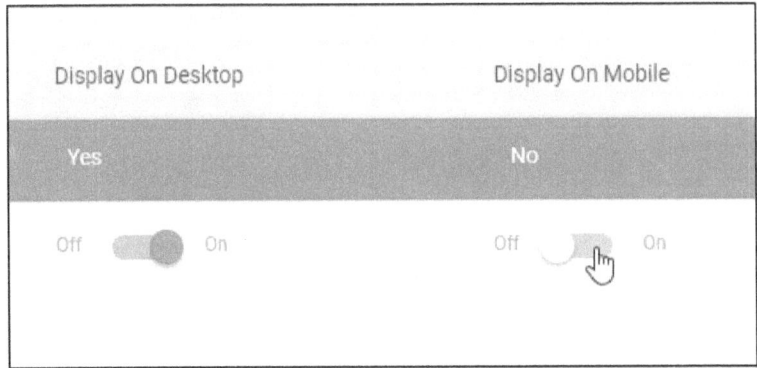

Figure 21: Choose Device(s)

Then select the pages and posts that you want this form to appear on by clicking on the Gear icon to the right,

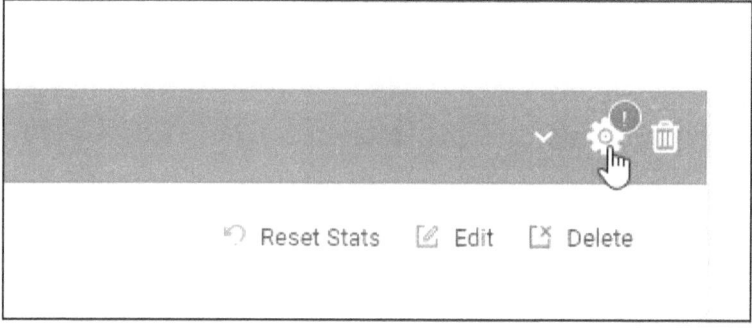

Figure 22: Select Your Targeting Options

You have a huge number of options to choose from to control exactly where your form is to appear on your website.

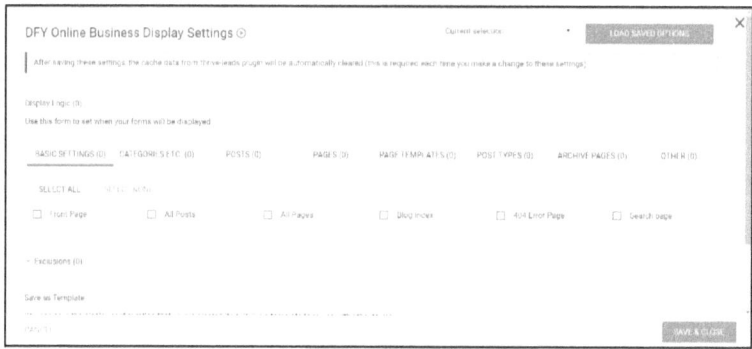

Figure 23: Specify Where the Form is to Appear

You have complete control over the pages and posts where your form will be displayed.

Internet Marketing Fast

Become a Thrive Expert

On the main screen under Basic Settings, you can Select All to display the form on all posts and all pages, you can check or uncheck any of front page, all posts, all pages, blog index, 404 error page and the search page or you can Select None and use one of the other tabs for finer control, right down to individual categories, posts, pages and more.

Figure 24: Basic Settings for Form Appearance

There are too many options to examine them all here, but they are pretty much self-explanatory if you work through them.

For example, if you select the Pages tab, you can select the individual pages that the form is to appear on. Of course, you must not also select All Pages under Basic Settings.

Figure 25: Select Individual Pages for Form Display

Save Your Choice as a Template

Finally, if you wish to apply these same settings to other forms, you can scroll down and save them as a template. This both saves work and ensures consistency.

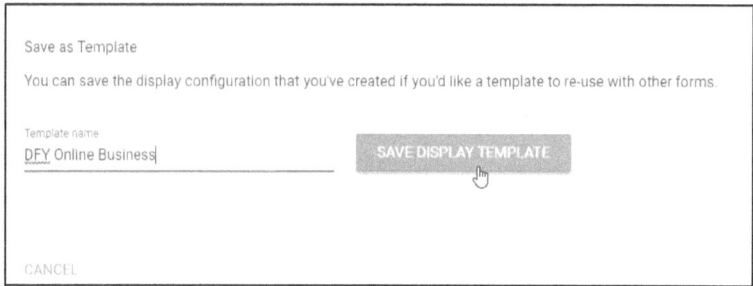

Figure 26: Save the Parameters as a Template

Lead Shortcodes

Lead Shortcodes allows you to create a specific kind of opt-in form and then to use its shortcode to add it to the posts or pages that you want it to appear on.

Internet Marketing Fast

Become a Thrive Expert

Unlike a Lead Group Form, Lead Shortcodes appear only on the specific posts and pages that you insert them on.

You still create them independently, but then insert the shortcodes on specific posts and pages.

Click the **Add New** button to create a new Lead Group.

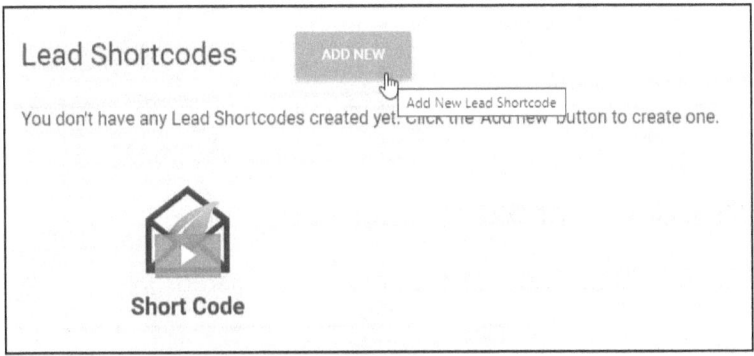

Figure 27: Add a New Lead Shortcode

Give the new Lead Shortcode a name that reflects your promotion.

Internet Marketing Fast

Become a Thrive Expert

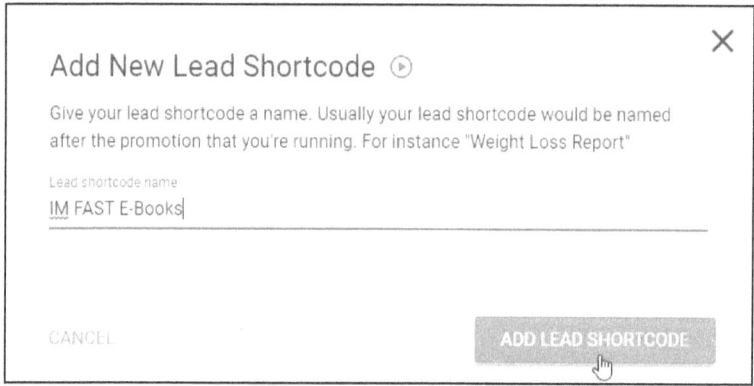

Figure 28: Give the Lead Shortcode a Name

Then click the **ADD LEAD SHORTCODE** button.

The new Lead Shortcode is created and listed.

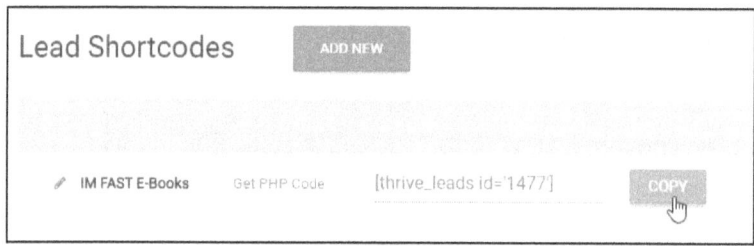

Figure 29: New Lead Shortcode Created

Next, you have to design the form that is to appear on the page when the shortcode is inserted. Click Edit to start this process.

Internet Marketing Fast

Become a Thrive Expert

Figure 30: Click Edit to Start the Form Design

Then click the **CREATE FORM** button.

Your forms will appear here.

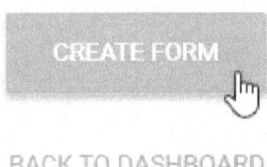

CREATE FORM

BACK TO DASHBOARD

Figure 31: Click the Create Form Button

Give your new form a name. Note that it already appears in the Lead Shortcode *IM FAST E-Books*, so there is no point in repeating this. One approach is to call it something like *Variation 1*, as you may wish to try other alternative appearances further down the track.

Internet Marketing Fast

Become a Thrive Expert

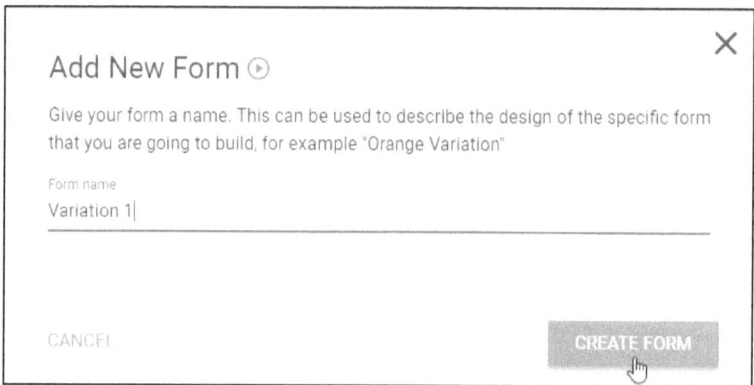

Figure 32: Give the Lead Shortcode Form a Name

The new form will be listed under the Lead Shortcode, and you can proceed to edit its design. You can also add more forms.

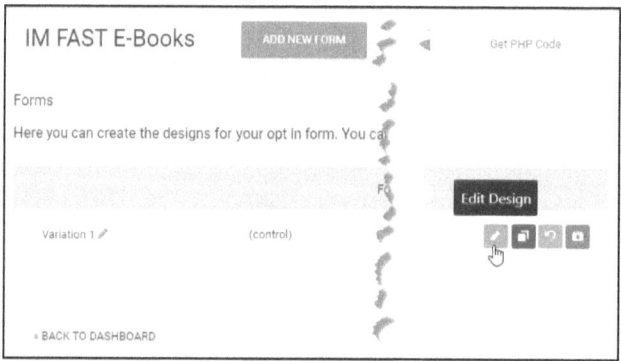

Figure 33: The New Lead Shortcode Form is Listed

Edit the Form's Design

Click on the **Edit Design** icon as shown above. This will load Thrive Architect for you to design the form.

Internet Marketing Fast

Start by selecting a template to use.

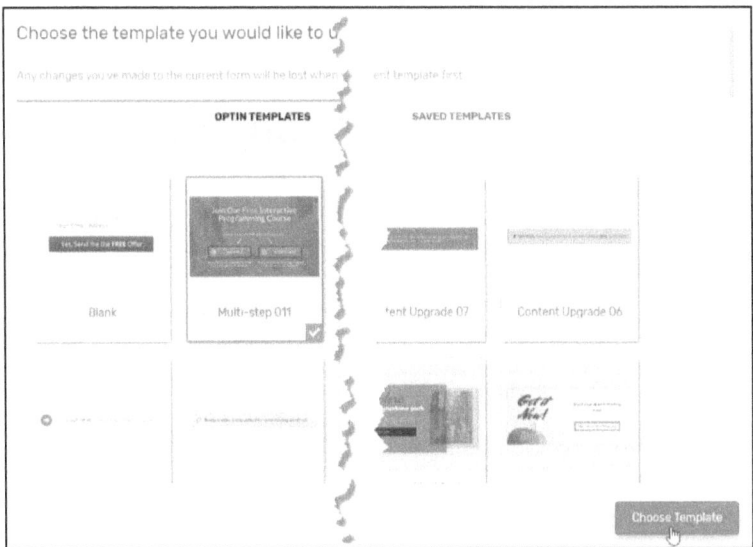

Figure 34: Select a Template for Your Form

Note that there are a lot of templates. Scroll down to see them all. Select one by clicking on it and then click the **Choose Template** button.

Figure 35: The Selected Template Can Be Modified

Using Thrive Architect, the selected template can be modified to suit your purposes.

Or you can select a different template.

Note that the process of connecting a Lead Gen element to your autoresponder is covered in *Book 6: Building Your Website*.

To make the lead appear on a post or page, copy its shortcode and insert it using Thrive Architect's Custom HTML element.

Internet Marketing Fast

Become a Thrive Expert

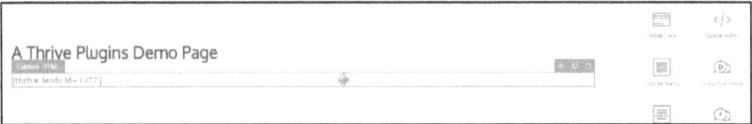

Figure 36: Add the Lead Shortcode to a Page

Then when the page is viewed it will replace the shortcode with the form that you have designed.

Figure 37: The Lead Shortcode Form is Shown

ThriveBoxes

ThriveBoxes allows you to design an opt-n and make it appear in specific posts or pages by inserting the generated short code.

Click the **Add New** button to add a new ThriveBox.

Internet Marketing Fast

Become a Thrive Expert

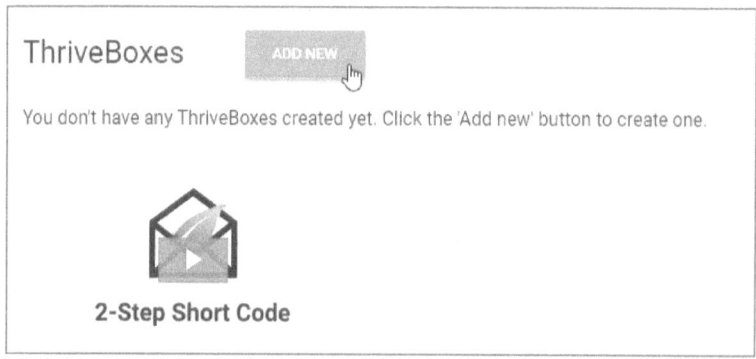

Figure 38: Add a New ThriveBox

Then give your new ThriveBox a name.

Figure 39: Give the ThriveBox a Name

The new ThriveBox is created and appears in a list. The next step is to create the form when the shortcode is inserted into a page. Click the **Edit** button.

Internet Marketing Fast

Become a Thrive Expert

Figure 40: Edit the ThriveBox

Then click the **Create Form** button.

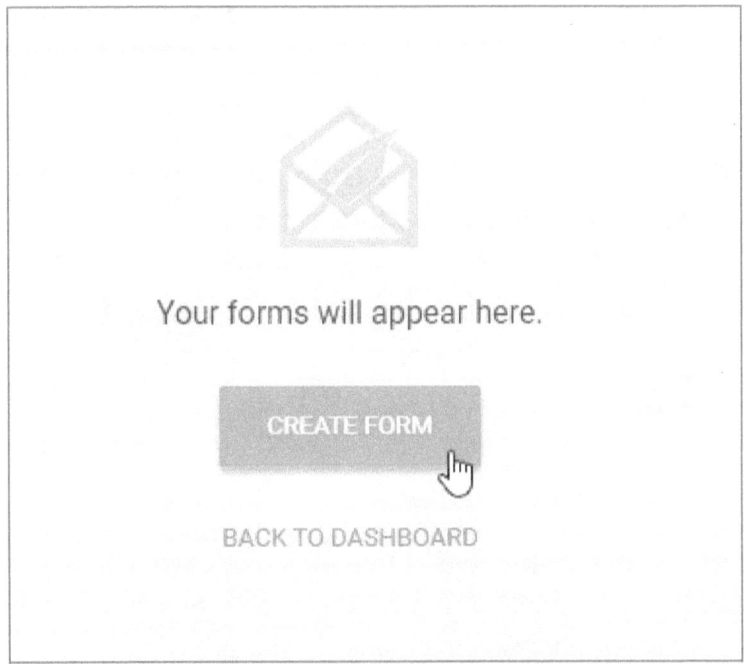

Figure 41: Click the Create ThriveBox Form Button

This will initiate the ThriveBox form design. Start off by giving the new form a name.

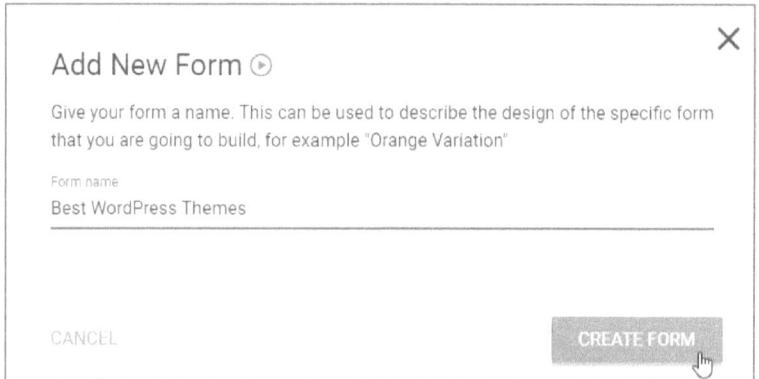

Figure 42: Give the New Form a Name

This will take you back to the list containing the ThriveBox, where you can edit the new form's design

Figure 43: Edit the New Form's Design

This will take you into a Thrive Architect page, where you can select a template to base this ThriveBox on, or create your own by choosing the blank template.

Scroll down to see the full range of templates.

Internet Marketing Fast

Become a Thrive Expert

Figure 44: Choose a ThriveBox Template

Figure 45: Copy the ThriveBox Shortcode

Signup Segue

The Signup Segue is used when you want to sign up people who are already on your mailing list to a new event.

While you could do that by sending them an email directing them to a sign-up form, that will seem silly to them as you already have their details. In fact, many will simply not be bothered with entering their details yet again.

The Signup Segue bypasses all that. You simply send them a link to your new event and if they say yes, their details are obtained from your mailing list in the background.

Prerequisites:

You will need to create the landing page that your visitor will be redirected to after they confirm. This will typically thank them for registering for your webinar (or whatever) and confirm their registration

You must of course have an autoresponder containing the list that you will be mailing to.

And you will need an API connection to your presentation platform, such as Zoom, GoToWebinar etc. You get the API credentials directly from that platform and enter them at Thrive Dashboard >> API Connections.

Alternatively, you could use your autoresponder as the destination platform in order get members' permission to move them from one list to another without having to re-enter their details.

Go to Thrive Dashboard >> Thrive Leads, scroll down to Signup Segue and click the **Add New** button.

Internet Marketing Fast

Become a Thrive Expert

Figure 46: Add New Signup Seque

Give your new Signup Segue a name and click the **Add Signup Segue** button.

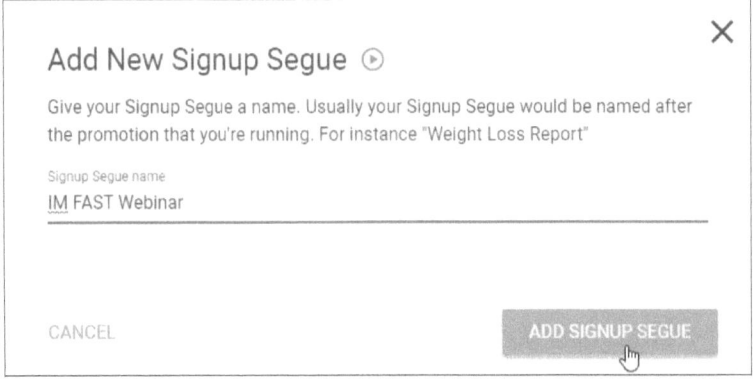

Figure 47: Click the Add Signup Segue Button

Your new Signup Segue is listed.

Now you must connect it to your destination platform. Start by clicking on *No Connections Set* under "Service".

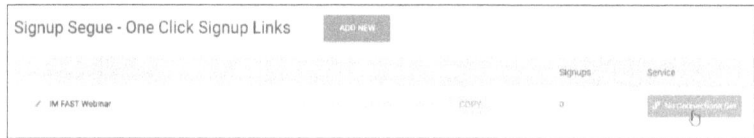

Figure 48: Click No Connections Set

The click the Add New button and select your destination platform.

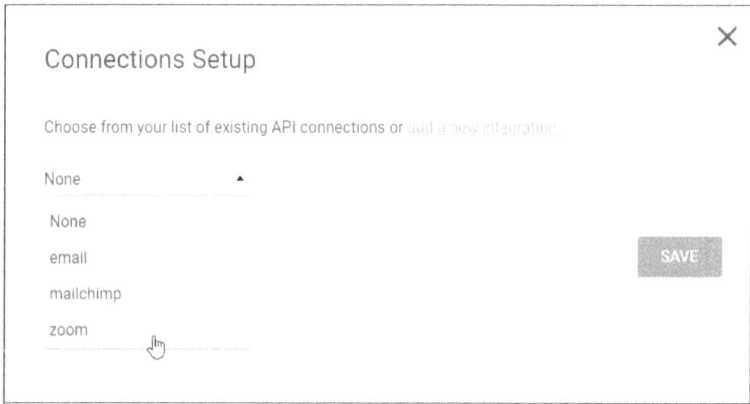

Figure 49: Select Your Webinar Platform

If you select a webinar platform, you will then be able to select a specific event.

If you selected your autoresponder instead, you would be able to select the mailing list and group to receive the transfer, as shown below.

Internet Marketing Fast

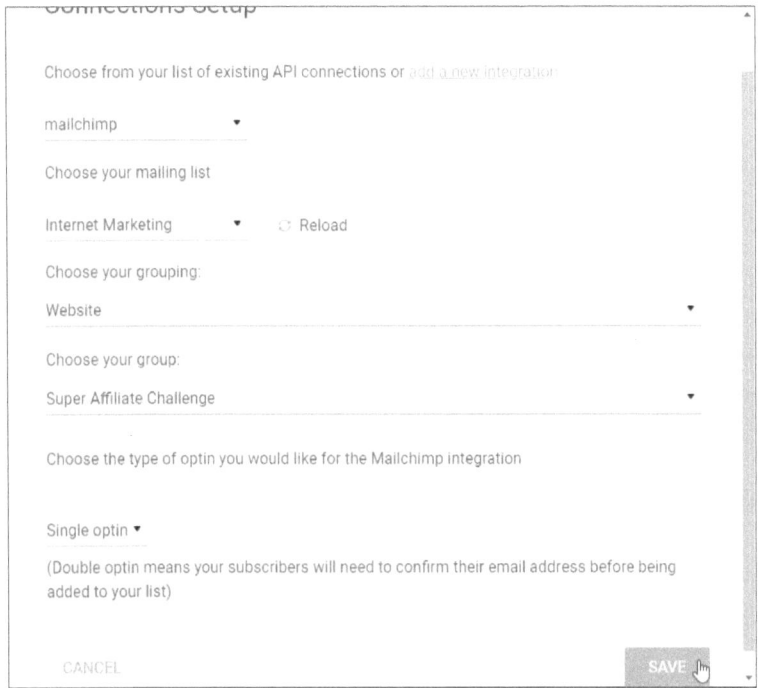

Figure 50: Choose Your Mailing List and Group

Then click the **Save** button.

This will return you to the Signup Segue list, which should now be showing your webinar platform or autoresponder name under the Service heading.

Click the **Redirect Settings** button to tell the Signup Segue where to take your visitor after signup. This will typically be a Thank You page, but there's no limit as to what you can show on it.

Internet Marketing Fast

Become a Thrive Expert

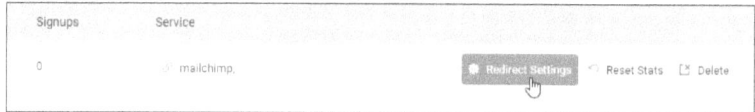

Figure 51: Select Your Redirect Destination

Choose the type of redirect you want. This will normally be a Single Redirect.

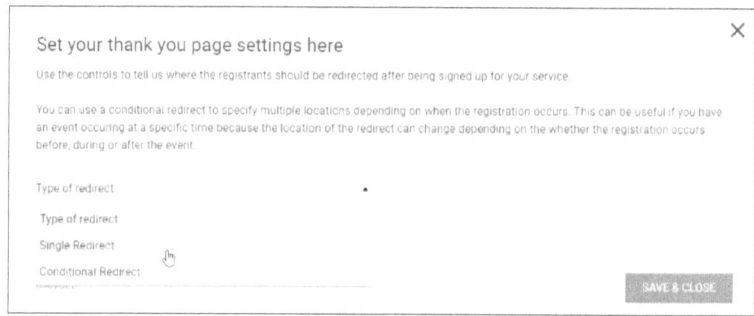

Figure 52: Select the Type of Redirect

Then find and select the Thank You page (which you will have created previously) that will be shown to your visitor after signup.

The Thank You page must already exist on your site.

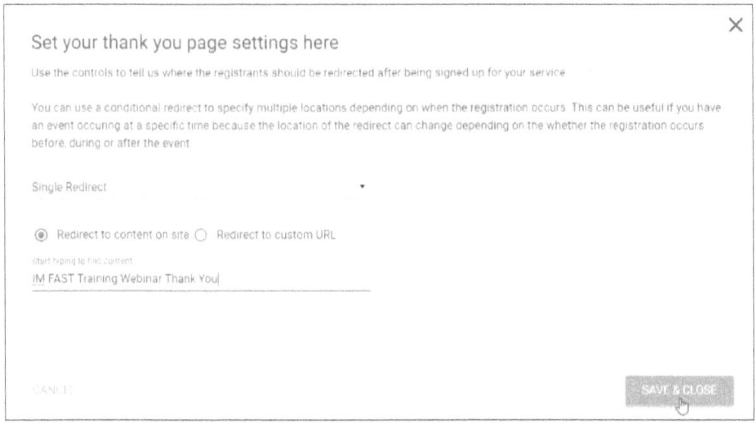

Figure 53: Select Signup Segue Thank You Page

Then click the **Save & Close** button.

To get the link to include in the email that you send to your list, go back to the Signup Segue list and copy the link.

Figure 54: Copy the Link

Now this link has generic tokens for your mailing list's name and email address, so you have to create your email inside your autoresponder and update the tokens there.

Here is the link pasted inside an email created in MailChimp:

Internet Marketing Fast

Become a Thrive Expert

https://superaffiliatechallenge.com/?post_type=tve_lead_1c_signup&p=1650&tl_name=[name]&tl_email=
[email]

Figure 55: The Link Generated by Signup Segue

This link contains the tokens [name] and [email]. You need to highlight each one in turn and replace it with the ones used by your autoresponder.

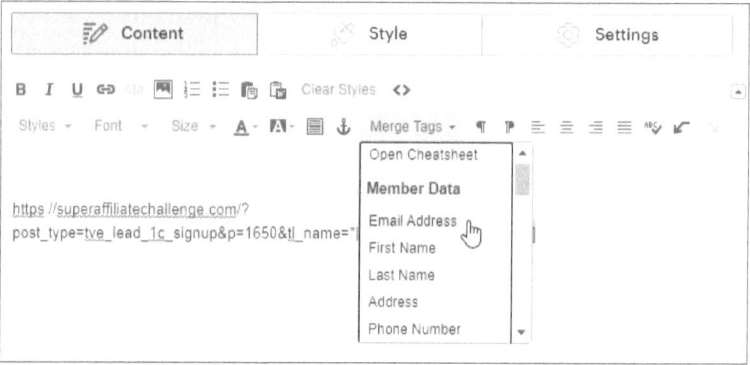

Figure 56: Replace the Name and Email Tokens

Thrive Quiz Builder

Quizzes are a great way to invite participation from your visitor and can lead to a sale.

For example, if you had a golfing website, you could construct your quiz around metrics that determine the factors that affect their swing, such as gender, age range, height and weight range and their handicap if they have one.

Internet Marketing Fast

Become a Thrive Expert

The answers could lead to a recommendation for a particular golf club driver and a link to purchase it.

Install Quiz Builder from the Thrive Product Manager.

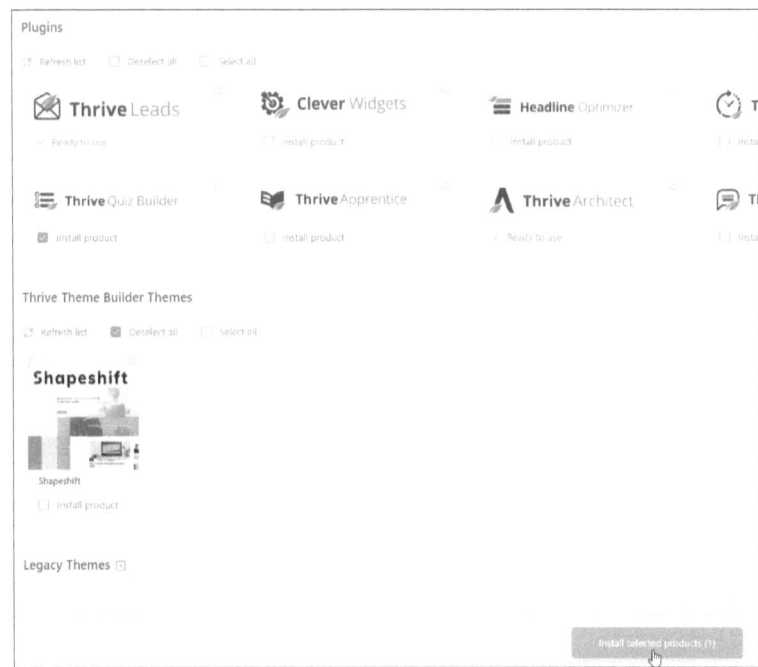

Figure 57: Select Quiz Builder in Thrive Product Manager

When Quiz Builder has been installed, you can access its dashboard from the Thrive dashboard.

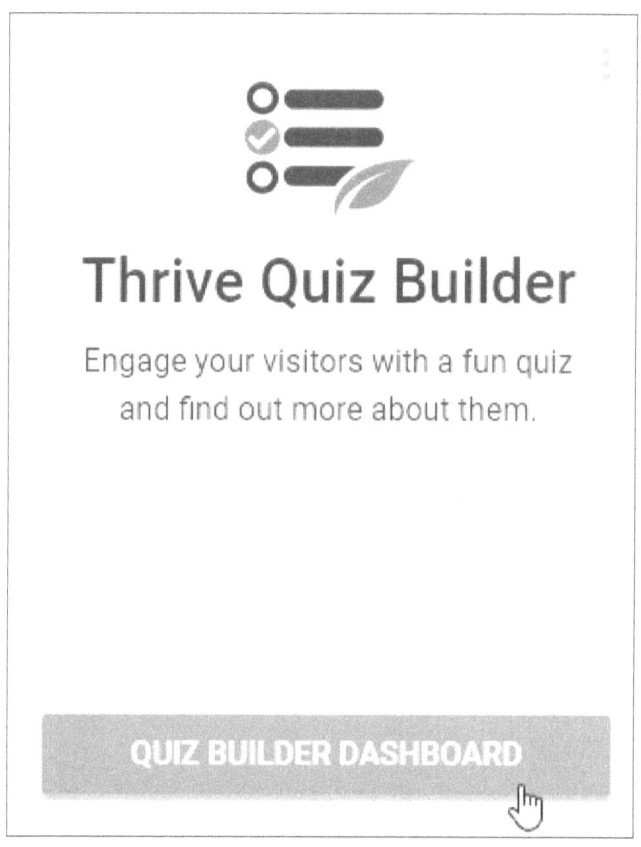

Figure 58: Select the Quiz Builder Dashboard

In the Quiz Builder dashboard, click the + button to add a new quiz.

Internet Marketing Fast

Become a Thrive Expert

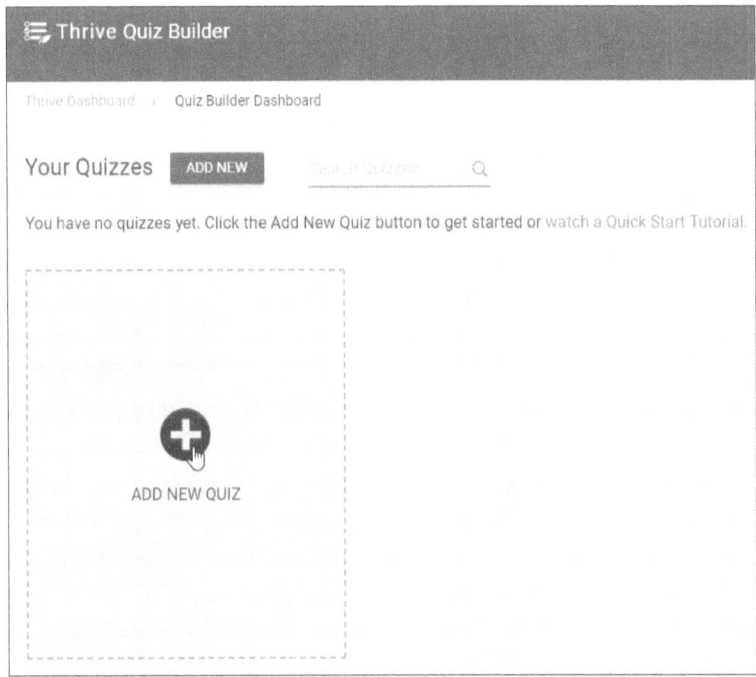

Figure 59: Click the + Button to Create a New Quiz

Then select a quiz template. I'm going to use the List Building template, as it allows me to display a result or recommendation based on the quiz answers and optionally require a opt-in before showing the result.

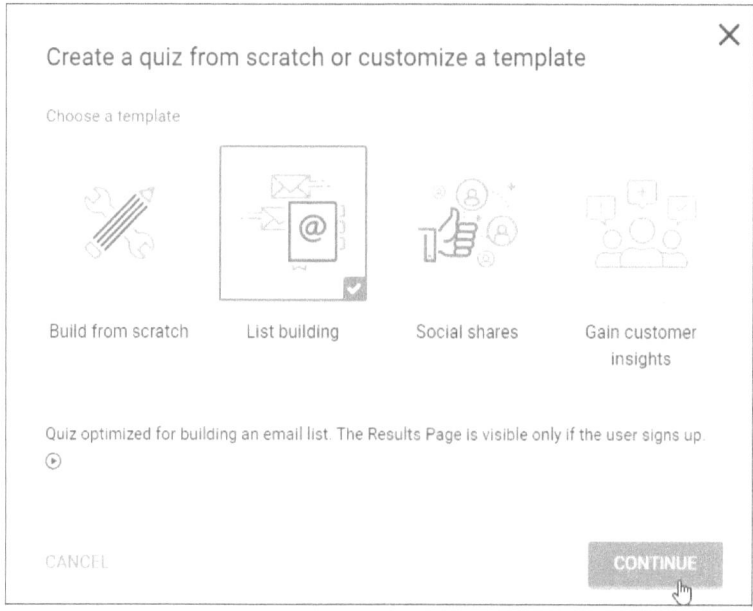

Figure 60: Select a Quiz Template

Give your quiz a name (internal use only) and click the **Continue** button.

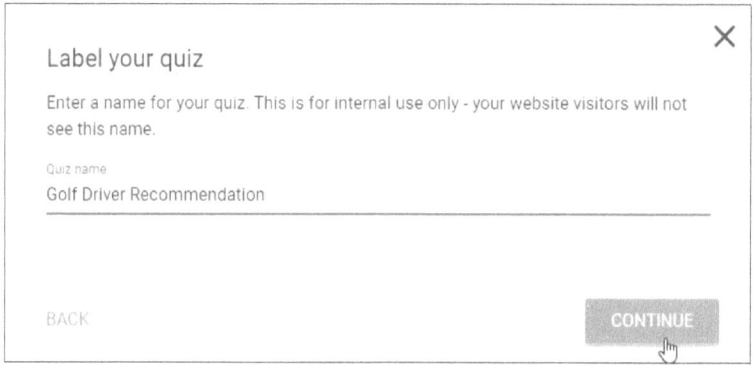

Figure 61: Give Your Quiz a Name

Internet Marketing Fast

Become a Thrive Expert

Choose your quiz type from

- Number
- Percentage
- Category
- Right/Wrong
- Survey

Which quiz type you choose will depend on the type of quiz you are running.

You can hover the mouse over each type to get a brief description of it.

In this case, the quiz will use the information gathered to recommend a particular golf club. This is called a Category Quiz.

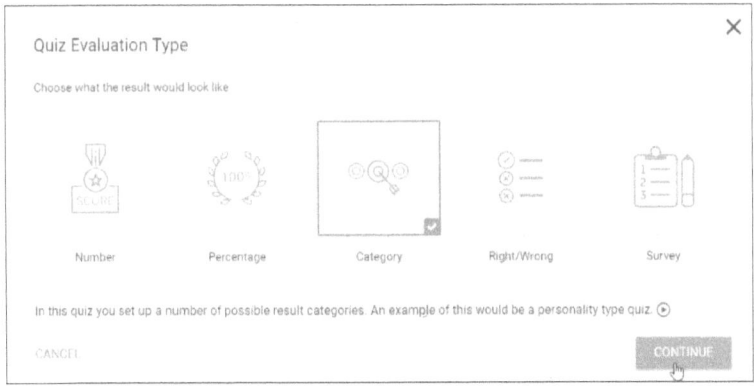

Figure 62: Choose Your Quiz Type

Next, add the categories, one of which will be displayed as the result. We are going to have three possible golf club drivers, rather imaginatively named Driver 1, Driver 2 and Driver 3.

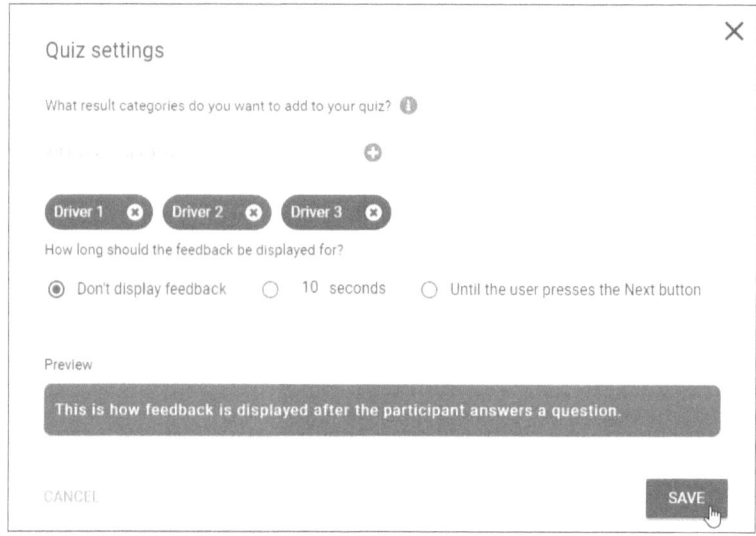

Figure 63: Add the Categories

Next, choose a style for your quiz. There are several to choose from and the style chosen governs the look of all four quiz pages.

- The splash page that introduces the quiz
- The quiz itself, with questions and, depending on the quiz type, answers
- The optional opt-in gate that asks the visitor to opt-in to your mailing list to get the result
- the Results page.

Internet Marketing Fast

Become a Thrive Expert

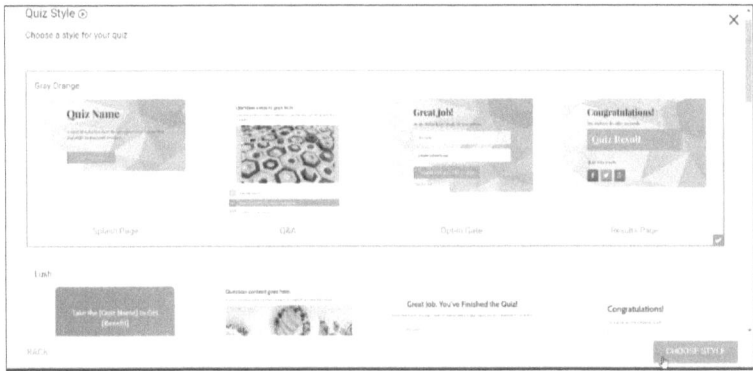

Figure 64: Choose a Quiz Style

Finally, edit the results page to reflect your quiz.

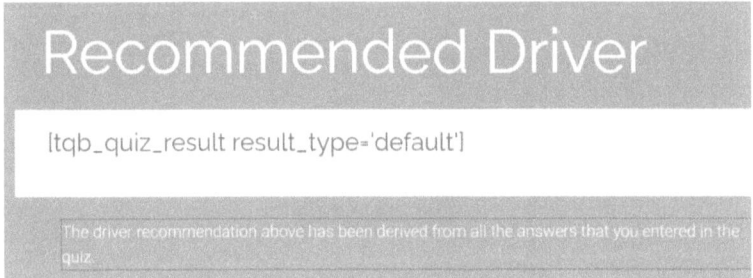

Figure 65: Edit the Results Page

The Thrive Quiz Builder dashboard will be showing the Quiz Structure, with the flow being:

Splash Page >> Quiz >> Opt-in Gate >> Results

Each of these can be edited.

Click on the Quiz page to add questions and optionally answers. You can move them around and drag and drop links to get the desired flow.

Internet Marketing Fast

Become a Thrive Expert

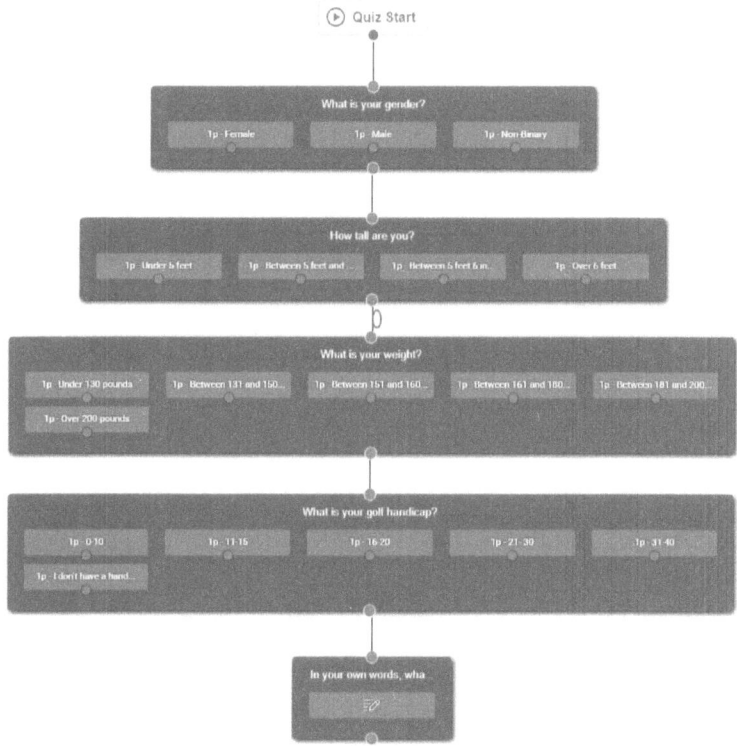

Figure 66: Quiz Flow

There are a number of options to be set for each question.

Select the question type from

- Multiple Choice with Buttons
- Multiple Choice with Images
- Open Ended Question

Internet Marketing Fast

Become a Thrive Expert

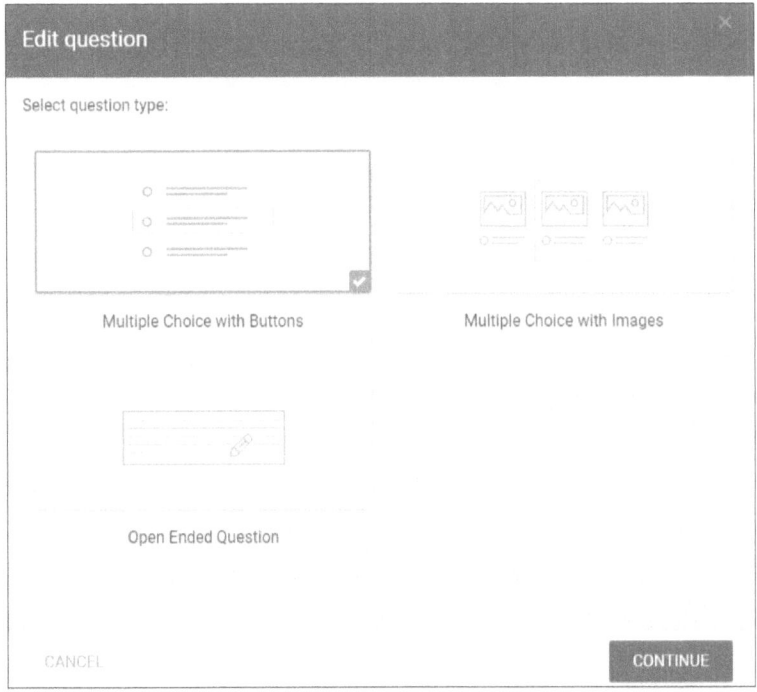

Figure 67: Select Question Type

Then enter your question and its possible answers.

Internet Marketing Fast

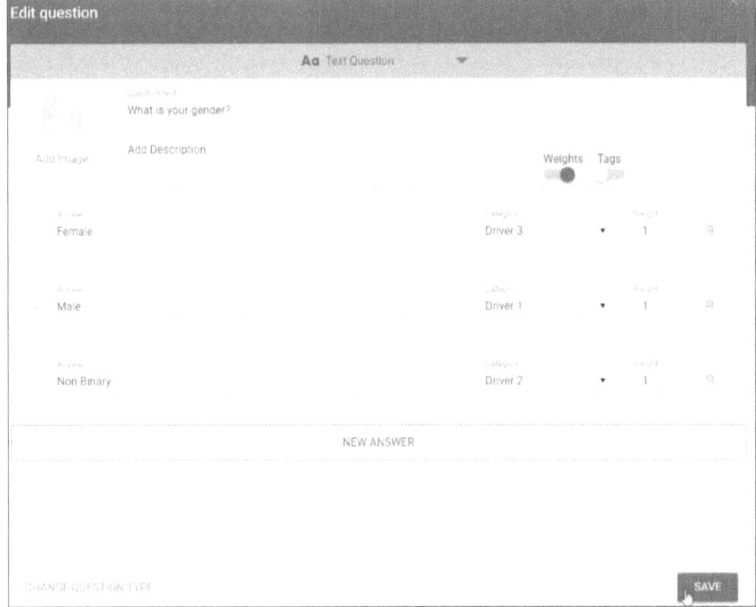

Figure 68: Enter Question and Answers

Because this is a Category quiz, you can enter which category will be associated with each answer.

You can also choose to add a weight to each answer to reflect how important the answer is in contributing to the final result.

Click on the Manage button and then the Edit icon to make changes to any of the pages in the Quiz Structure.

When you've finished, copy the Quiz Shortcode from the upper right in the Quiz Structure page. Insert the shortcode into any page where you want the quiz to appear.

Internet Marketing Fast

Become a Thrive Expert

Thrive Ultimatum

Thrive Ultimatum is Thrive's scarcity plugin, designed to use the power of FOMO (Fear of Missing Out) to persuade visitors to take up your offer.

Install Ultimatum from the Thrive Product Manager.

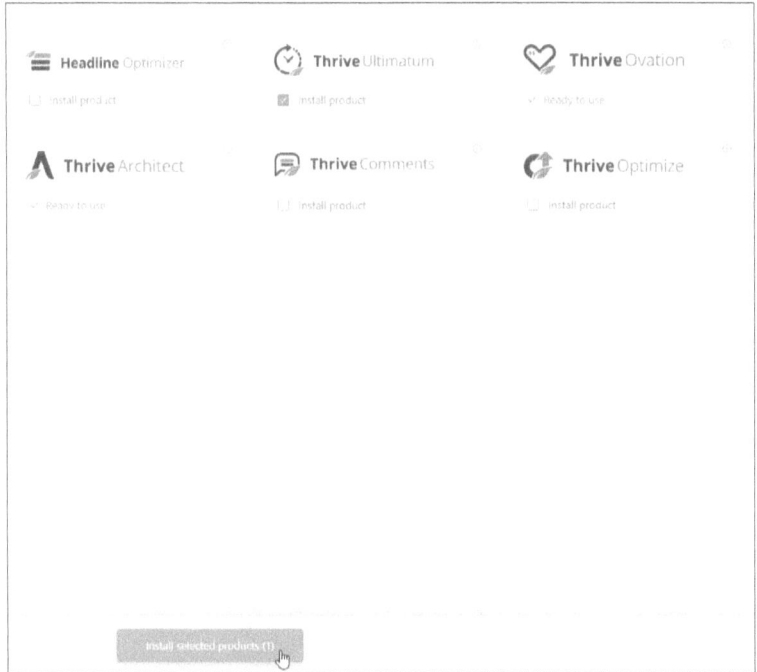

Figure 69: Install Thrive Ultimatum

Go to the Thrive Dashboard and load the Thrive Ultimatum Dashboard.

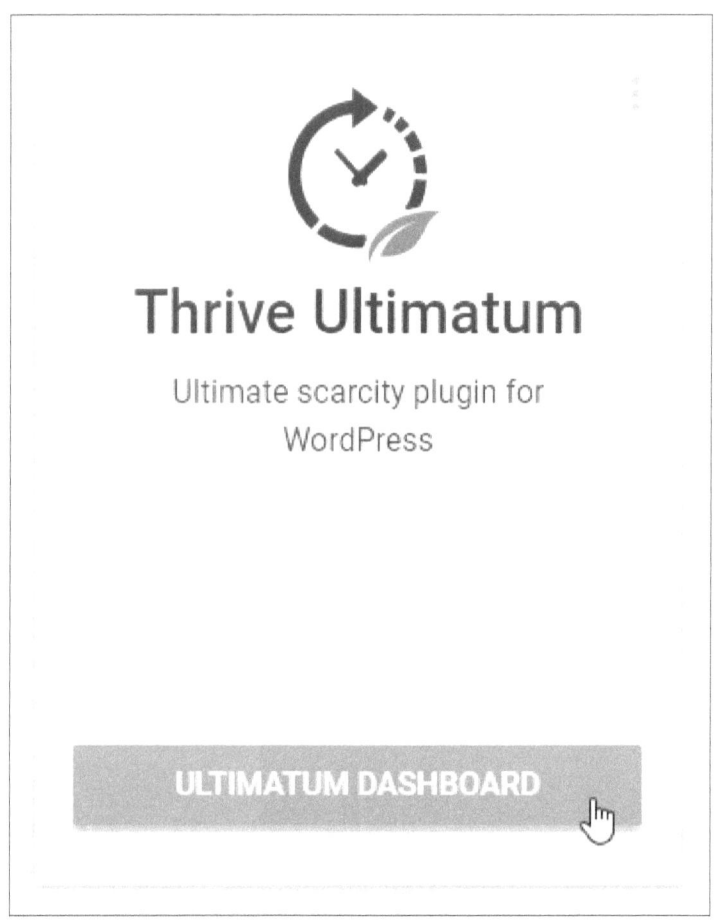

Figure 70: Load the Ultimatum Dashboard

Once you're in the Ultimatum Dashboard, click on the + button to create a new campaign.

There are several campaign types to choose from and variables to be configured for each type.

Internet Marketing Fast

Become a Thrive Expert

You should experiment with each type to tailor it to your particular needs.

For this example, we are going to build a *7 day offer* campaign.

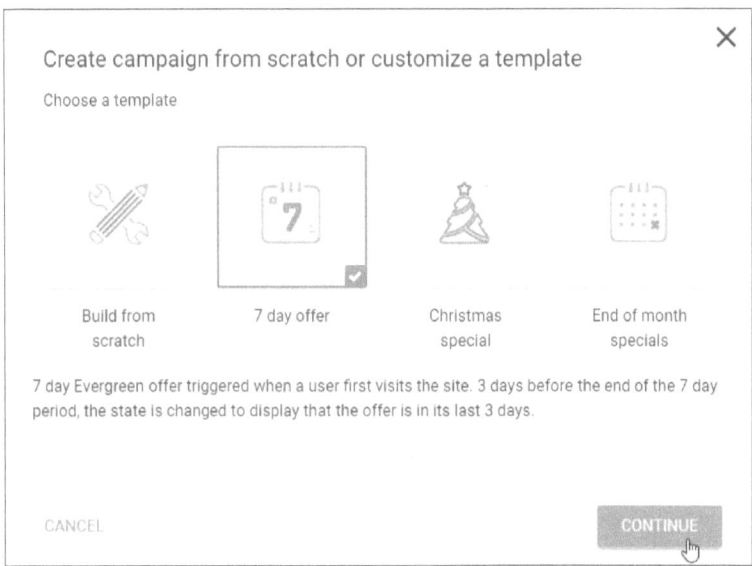

Figure 71: Choose Your Campaign Type

Give your campaign a name. This is for internal use only and will not be seen by your visitors.

Then click the **Continue** button.

Internet Marketing Fast

Become a Thrive Expert

Figure 72: Name Your Ultimatum Campaign

The next step is to select a display mode. This is where you choose whereabouts on your website this campaign is to be displayed.

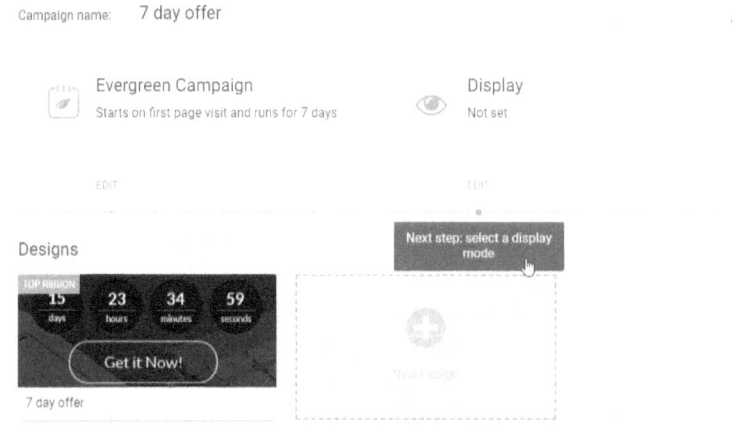

Figure 73: Select a Display Mode

For example, you could choose to display the campaign on the front page and on all blog posts.

Internet Marketing Fast

Become a Thrive Expert

Note that Evergreen Campaign has been chosen by default. This means that the campaign will run for 7 days for each user from the time they first see it.

You can also have date-driven and recurring campaigns.

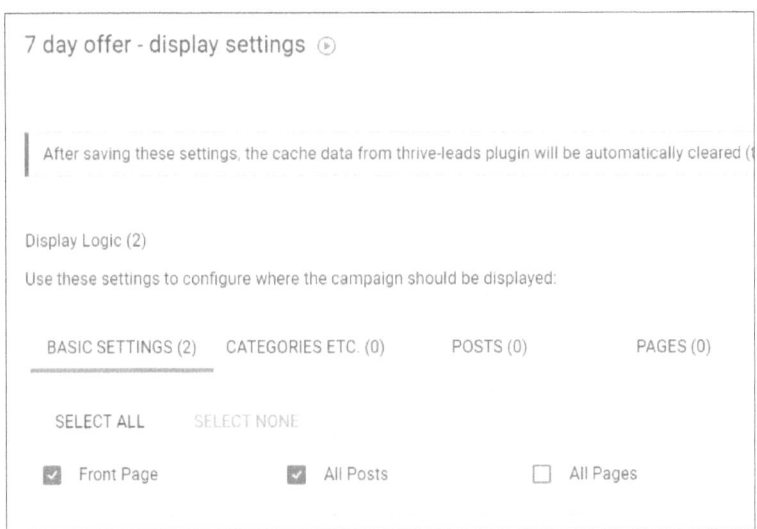

Figure 74: Choose Where the Campaign is Displayed

If you scroll down, you will see similar settings that govern where the campaign should not be displayed.

So if you selected All Pages in the upper section and Front Page in the lower, then the campaign would be shown on all pages except the front page.

Click the Save & Close button when you've made your selections.

Internet Marketing Fast

Select the lockdown options for a date-driven or recurring campaign.

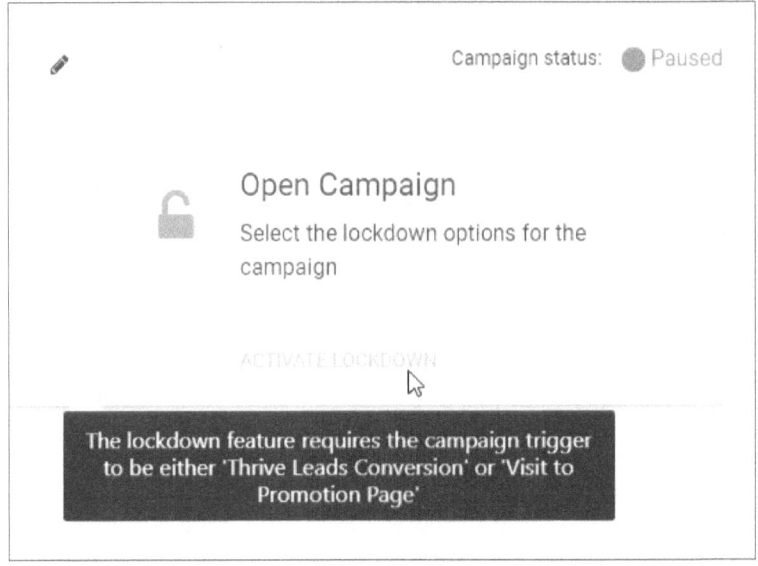

Figure 75: Select the Lockdown Options

The button will not be activated for an Evergreen Campaign.

Next, you can design the look of your countdown timer.

Internet Marketing Fast

Become a Thrive Expert

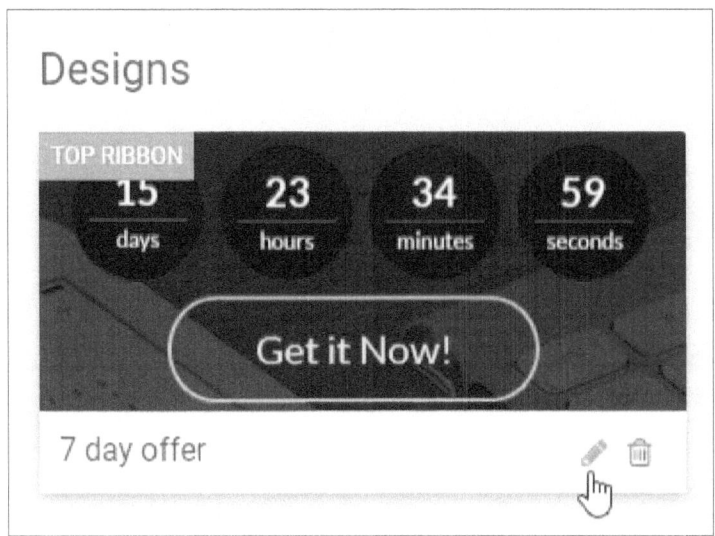

Figure 76: Design the Look of Your Countdown Timer

Click on the edit icon to bring up the timer ribbon in Thrive Architect.

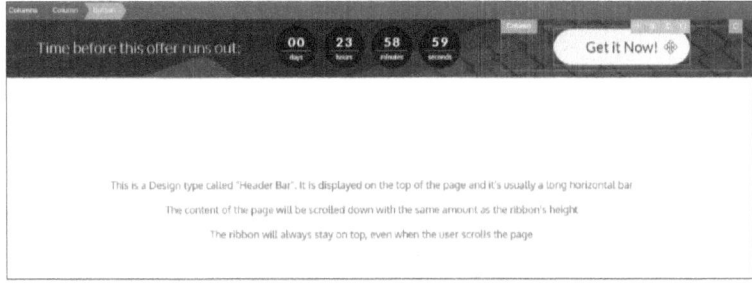

Figure 77: Modify the Ribbon Using Thrive Architect

The ribbon will be displayed at the top of each page that fits the criteria selected when you defined the display mode.

Internet Marketing Fast

Become a Thrive Expert

The ribbon stays in place as the visitor scrolls down the page, so that it is a constant reminder to take action.

You can edit any aspect of the ribbon, including colors, text and button link.

You would probably edit the wording to identify the offer and the button to link to your offer page.

You can have a different design to be displayed for the last 3 days of the campaign for the visitor.

Click the + sign in the lower right-hand corner and select Last 3 Days.

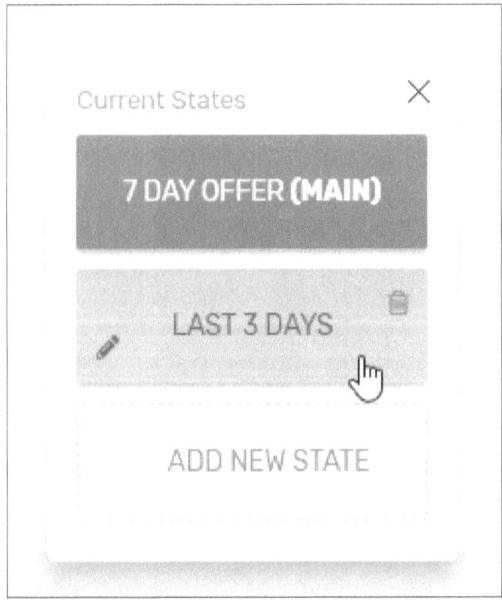

Figure 78: Change the Design for the Last 3 Days

Internet Marketing Fast

Become a Thrive Expert

You could make changes to the display to increase the sense of urgency for the visitor.

The campaign's timeline shows a visual representation of the 7-day period for each visitor.

Figure 79: Showing the Campaign's Timeline

Now go back to the Dashboard, where you can start the campaign when ready.

Click on the arrow to start the campaign.

Internet Marketing Fast

Become a Thrive Expert

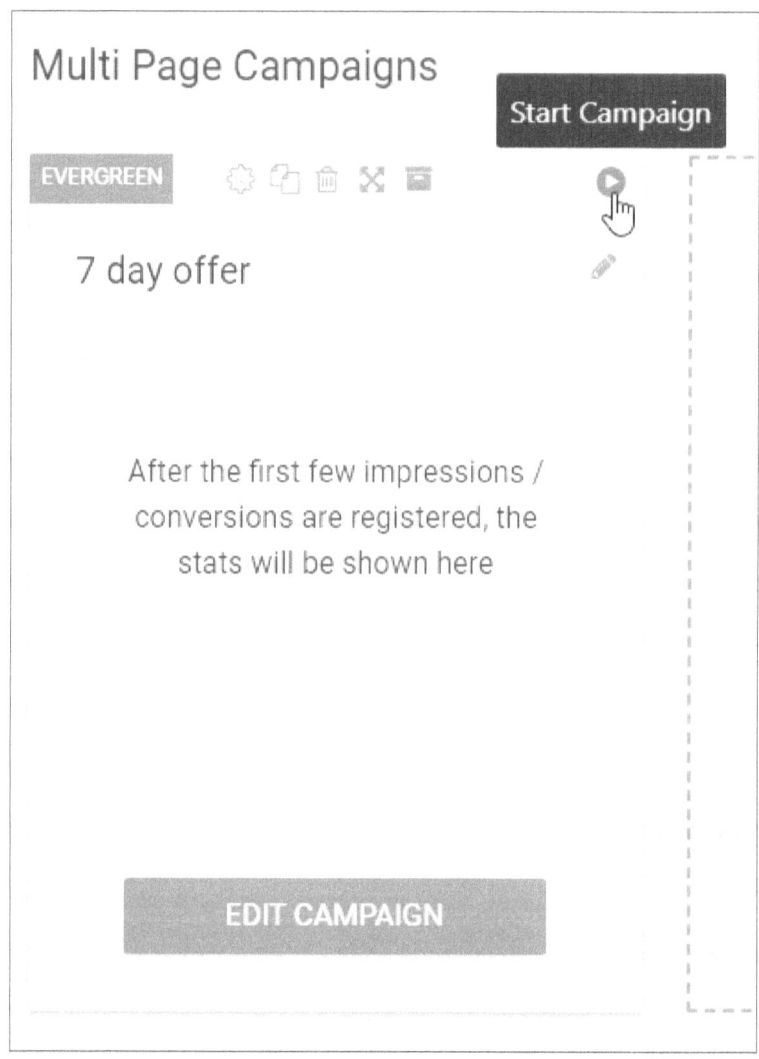

Figure 80: Start the Ultimatum Campaign

Internet Marketing Fast

As soon as the campaign has started, the countdown ribbon will appear to your visitor at the top of the pages that you selected for it to be shown.

Figure 81: The Campaign Has Started

Don't forget to explore the other types of campaign that you can run, namely *Fixed Dates* and *Recurring*.

Thrive Ovation

Thrive Ovation is a testimonials management plugin.

It enables you to collect testimonials from your customers and then display them wherever you like using a shortcode. You can choose from several testimonial formats.

As with other Thrive plugins, you download Thrive Ovation from the Thrive product manager. You can then find it in the Thrive dashboard.

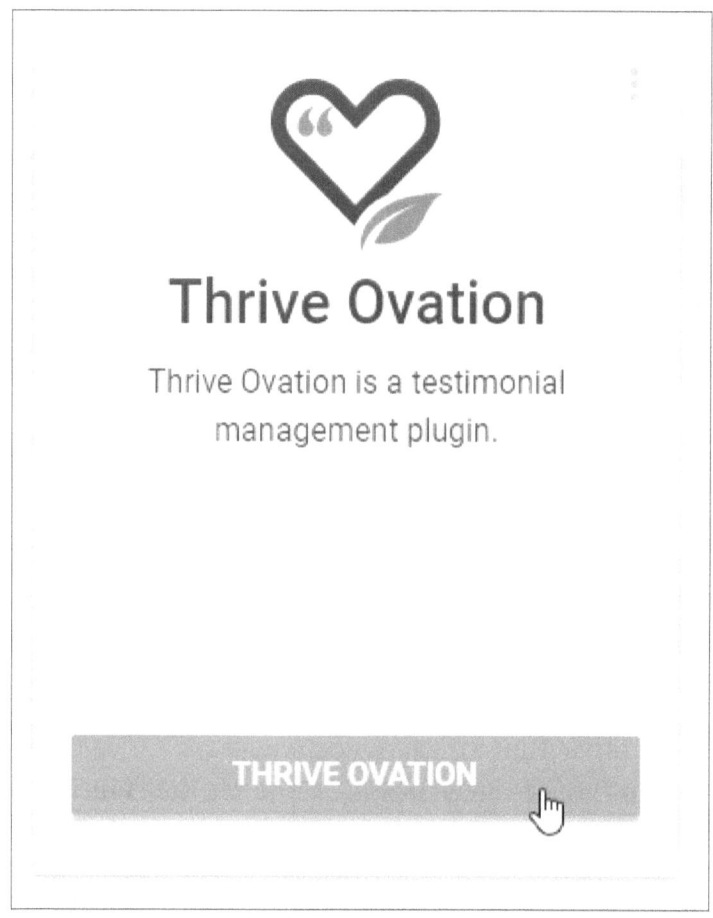

Figure 82: Click to Access Thrive Ovation

There are two aspects to Thrive Ovation – capturing testimonials and displaying them.

You can capture testimonials in different ways. For example, you can direct customers to a page that you create using Thrive Architect.

Internet Marketing Fast

Become a Thrive Expert

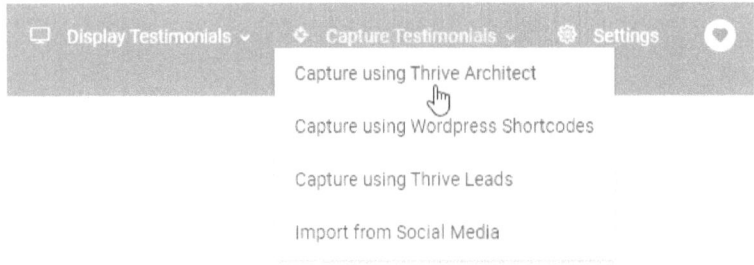

Figure 83: Capture Testimonials with Architect

Clicking on any of the options will play a short video explaining the basics for that option.

You can build a Capture page (which you could refer new customers to) using Thrive Architect.

It can be a normal page, a blog post or a landing page.

Because you've installed Ovation, some new options appear in the Thrive Architect's elements list.

They are at the end of the list, under the heading *Thrive Integrations*.

Internet Marketing Fast

Become a Thrive Expert

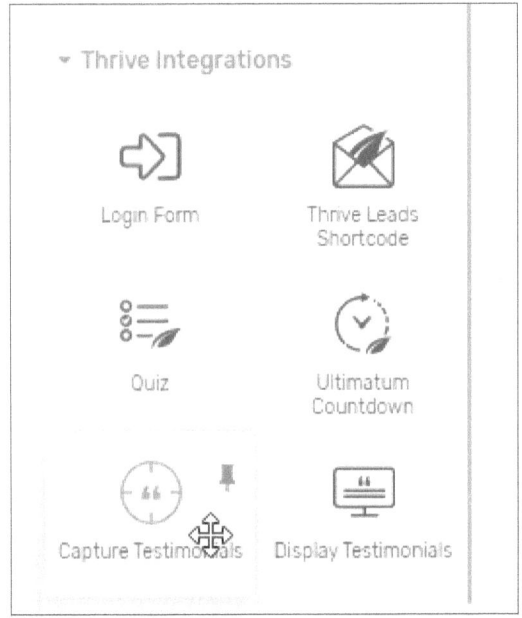

Figure 84: The Capture Testimonials Element

When you add the Capture Testimonials element to a page, you can customize its appearance by selecting a template.

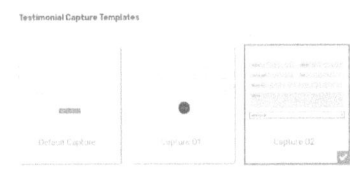

Figure 85: Choose a Capture Testimonial Template

This puts a basic Testimonial Capture form on the page.

Internet Marketing Fast

Because it's in Thrive Architect, you can add any additional text or images that you want on the page.

For example, you would identify the product that you are seeking the testimonial for, tell the customer how much you value their opinion and so on.

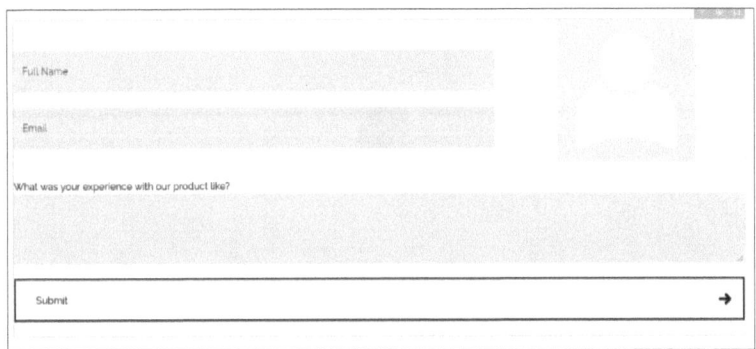

Figure 86: Basic Page from Ovation Template

This page requests name, email address and statement (the actual testimonial) optionally allows for an image upload and has a **Submit** button.

You can modify any of these fields and add new ones.

In the left-hand menu for *Capture Testimonials*, click the **Form Settings** button.

Internet Marketing Fast

Become a Thrive Expert

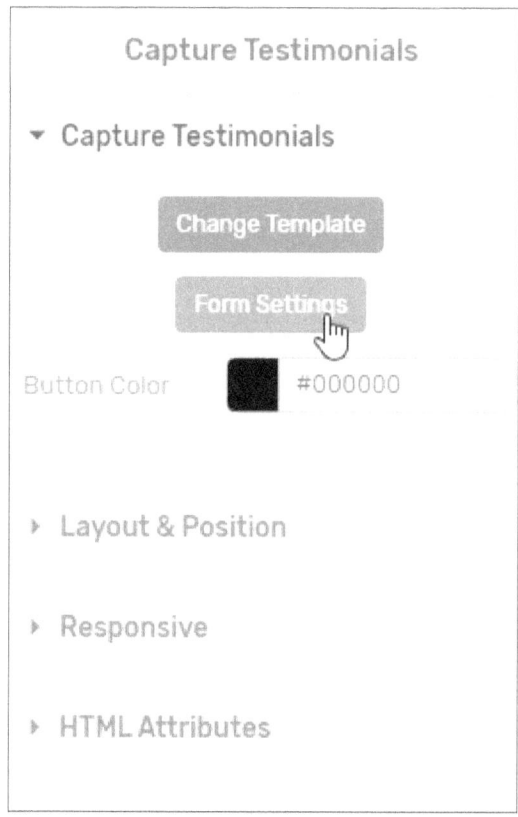

Figure 87: Click the Form Settings Button

From here, you have full control over what appears on the form, including asking any additional questions that would be relevant to the product or service being reviewed.

Internet Marketing Fast

Become a Thrive Expert

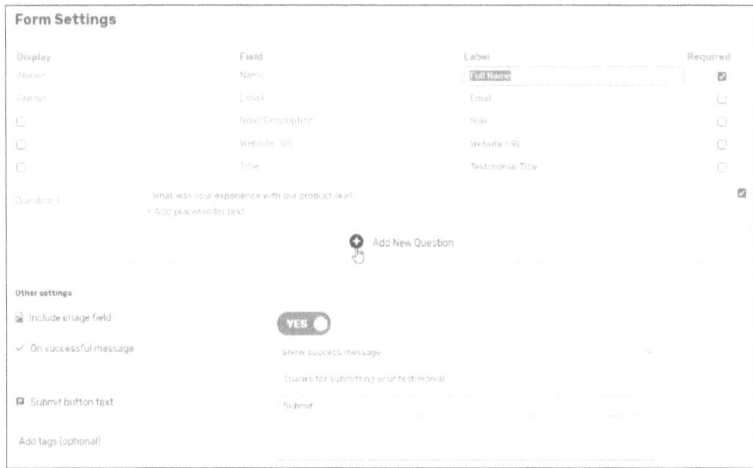

Figure 88: Edit the Ovation Form's Fields

Once customers start submitting testimonials, they will appear in the testimonial list in the Thrive Ovation dashboard.

You can edit any of the testimonials appearing in this list. When a testimonial is ready, set it to *Ready to Display*.

Internet Marketing Fast

Become a Thrive Expert

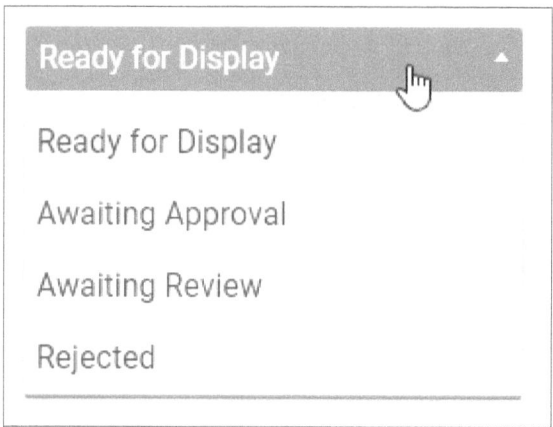

Figure 89: Set Testimonial Ready for Display

You can then create a new page with Thrive Architect and display any of the testimonials on it.

Select the *Display Testimonials* element from the list of elements under *Thrive Integrations*.

Internet Marketing Fast

Become a Thrive Expert

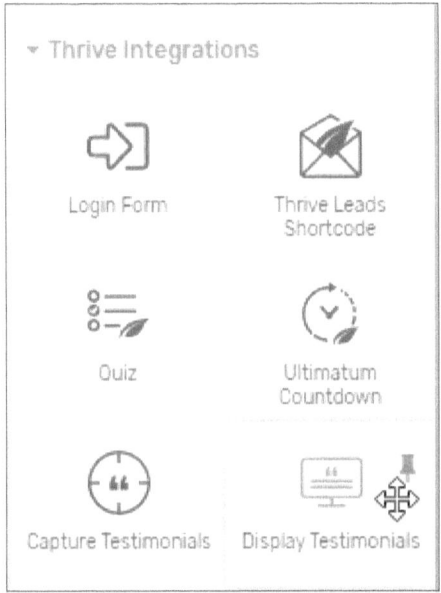

Figure 90: Select the Display Testimonials Element

Then click the **+ Select Testimonials** button and choose one of the many templates that govern the look and feel of the display.

Figure 91: Select a Display Template

Then scroll down and click the **Save** button.

Select from the list of testimonials ready to display. Your chosen testimonial is displayed in the template format that you selected.

Internet Marketing Fast

Become a Thrive Expert

FUNKY COOL INTERIORS

EMMA MORGAN

My overall experience was great, I can't recommend
Phil enough

I love my website, it is awesome. Phil added
everything I asked for and made it very user friendly

Phil was in contact with me often to make sure it was

Figure 92: Testimonial Display

Clever Widgets

Widgets normally appear in the sidebar for all posts.

Thrive Clever Widgets add extra functionality by specifying
conditions for which the widget will or will not be displayed.

You could use this, for example, to display different offer
promotions for different posts.

Internet Marketing Fast

Become a Thrive Expert

Go to the Thrive Product Manager and install Clever Widgets.

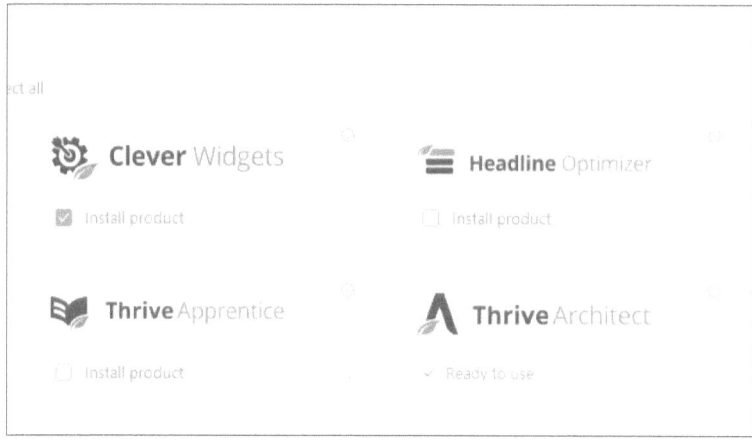

Figure 93: Install Clever Widgets

Go to Appearance >> Widgets.

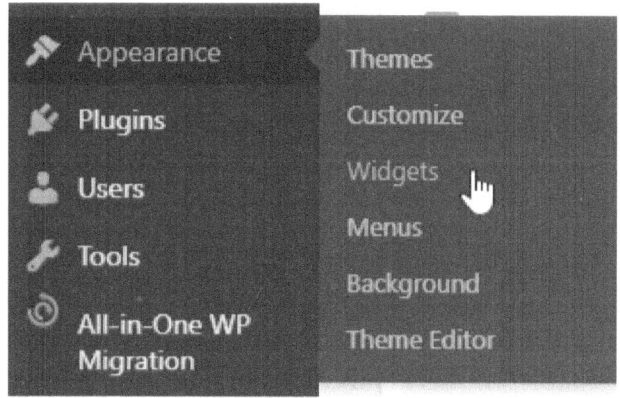

Figure 94: Select Widgets

Internet Marketing Fast

Become a Thrive Expert

Any widget that you have set to appear, now has an additional function *Thrive Widget Display Options*.

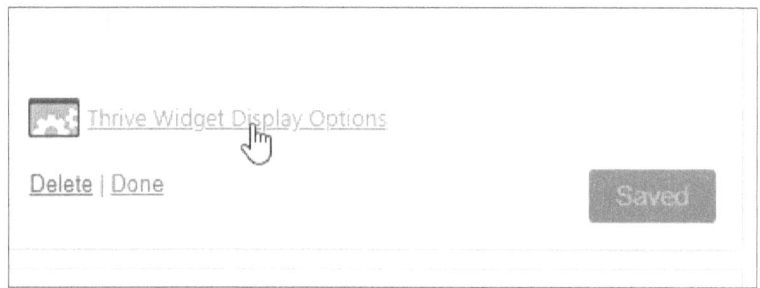

Figure 95: Select Thrive Widget Display Options

This allows you to specify the conditions under which that particular widget will be displayed.

There are many options to chose from, ranging from broad categories right down to individual posts.

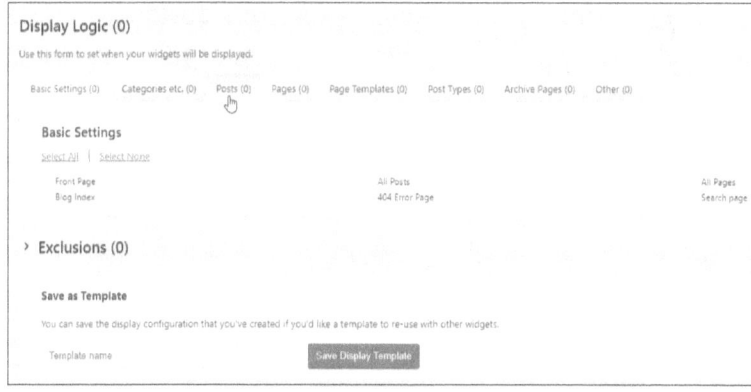

Figure 96: Control When Widget is Displayed

Internet Marketing Fast

Become a Thrive Expert

Headline Optimizer

Install Headline Optimizer from the Thrive Product Manager.

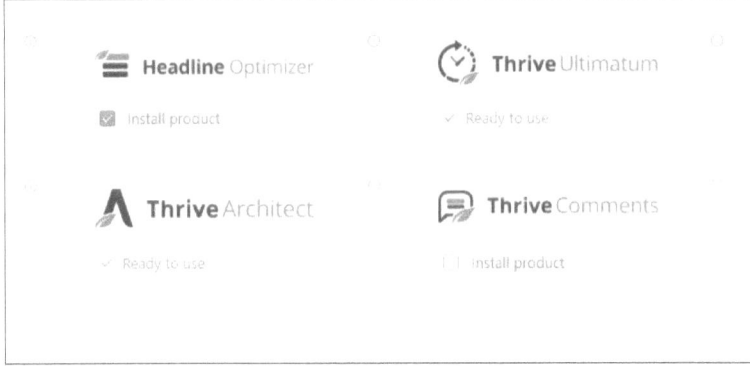

Figure 97: Install Headline Optimizer

The idea behind Headline Optimizer is to make it easy for you to try alternative headlines for your posts and pages and automatically choose the ones that give the best result.

Load Thrive Headline Optimizer from the Thrive Dashboard.

Internet Marketing Fast

Become a Thrive Expert

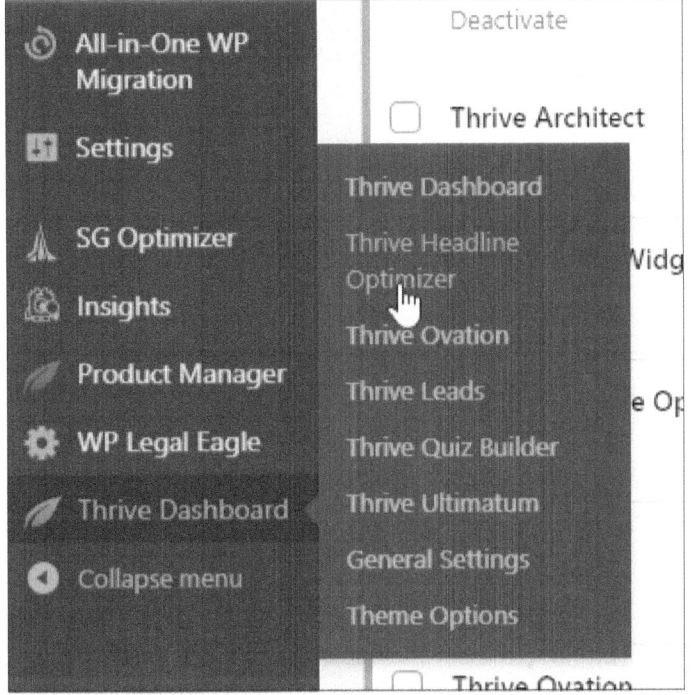

Figure 98: Load Thrive Headline Optimizer

You can watch the *Getting Started* video or click the **Add New** button to specify the posts or pages to optimize.

Internet Marketing Fast

Become a Thrive Expert

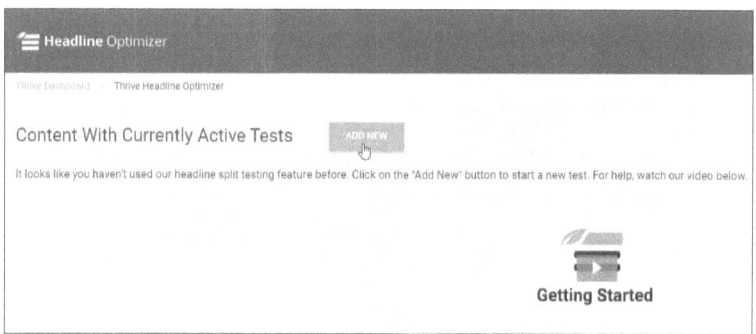

Figure 99: Click the Add New Button

When you click Add New, you will see a list of all the posts and/or pages from your site and can choose one or more to test alternate headlines for.

Internet Marketing Fast

Become a Thrive Expert

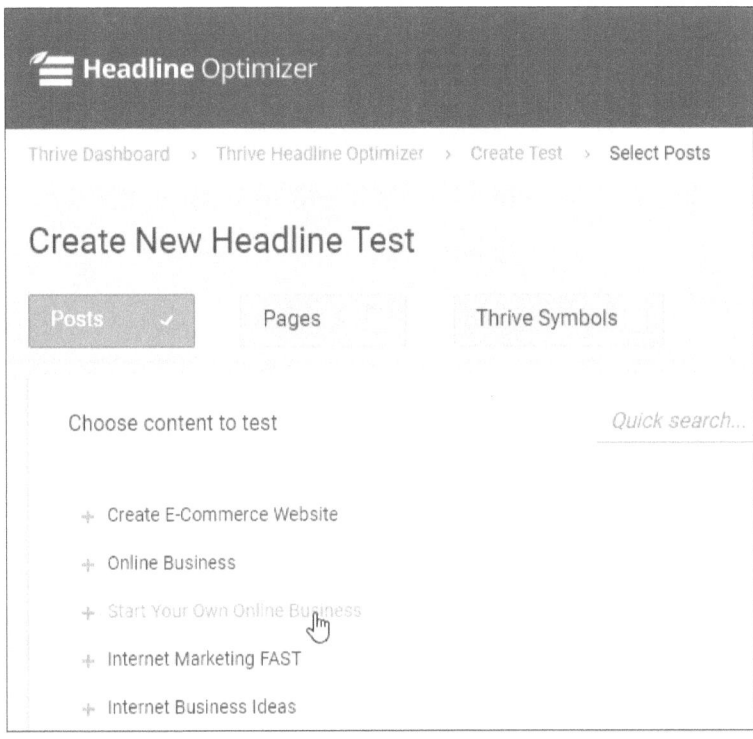

Figure 100: Choose Posts or Pages to Test

The posts and/or pages selected move to the *List of Content to be Tested.*

Internet Marketing Fast

Become a Thrive Expert

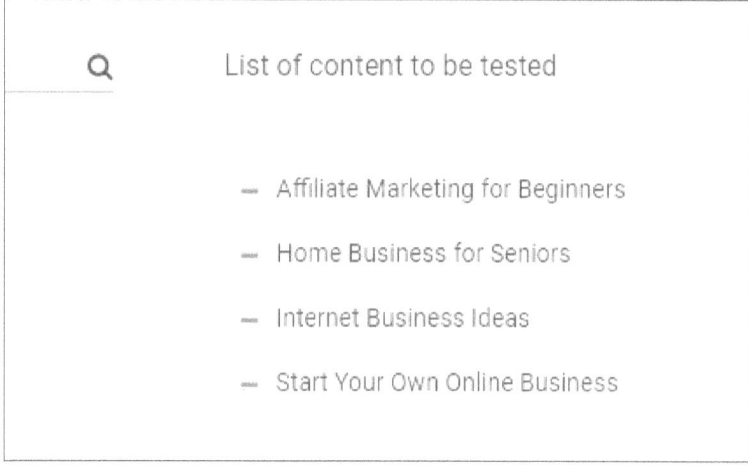

Figure 101: Content to be Tested

You can click on any headline in the list to move it back.

Click the **Save and Continue** button to move on to entering alternative headlines.

You can create as many variations of a headline as you want, but it's probably best to stick to 2 or 3. Press Enter to create a new variation and Tab to move to the next post or page in the list.

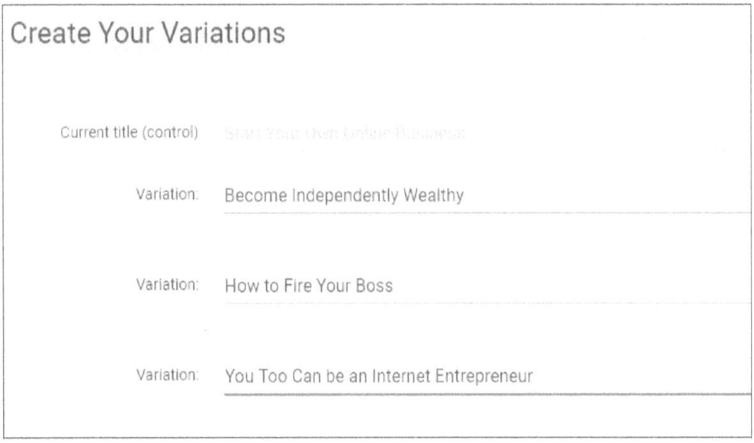

Internet Marketing Fast

Become a Thrive Expert

Figure 102: Create Your Variations

Click the **Next Step: Determine Test Criteria** button when you're done.

This shows the default test criteria.

Set Your Test Criteria

After saving these settings, the cache data from thrive-leads plugi

Engagement settings
We use certain signals to determine if a user is engaged or not.

Use default engagement settings   Off ⬤ On

Automatic winner settings

Enable automatic winner settings   Off ⬤ On

Here you can set the conditions by which a headline will be c

Minimum engagements	200	
Minimum duration	14	Days
Chance to beat original	97.5	%

Figure 103: Setting Test Criteria

The defaults are fine, so I suggest that you leave them as is, at least initially. When you get more experience with how the Thrive Headline Optimizer works, you can try some experimentation.

Click the **Start Test** button.

You will then see a summary of the running tests and, as time goes by, the results of those tests.

Figure 104: Optimizer Test Summary

At the end of the predefined period, the headline with the most engagement will be automatically selected as the winner and will be used.

Alternatively, you can click on the test, set it to complete and choose a winner manually.

Thrive Apprentice

Thrive Apprentice allows you to build multi-media training courses directly into your website.

Install it from the Thrive Product Manager.

Internet Marketing Fast

Become a Thrive Expert

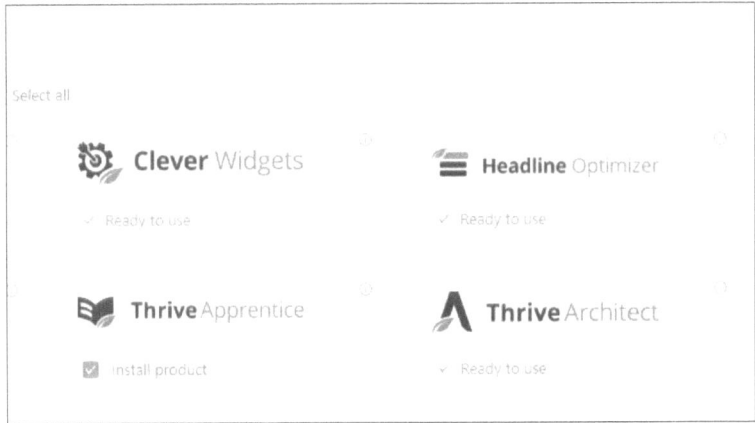

Figure 105: Install Thrive Apprentice

To start building your course, click on Thrive Dashboard and then Apprentice Dashboard.

Internet Marketing Fast

Become a Thrive Expert

Figure 106: Click Apprentice Dashboard

The first thing you will do is select the page to host your training course(s) if you've already created it or (more likely) name and create it now.

Internet Marketing Fast

Become a Thrive Expert

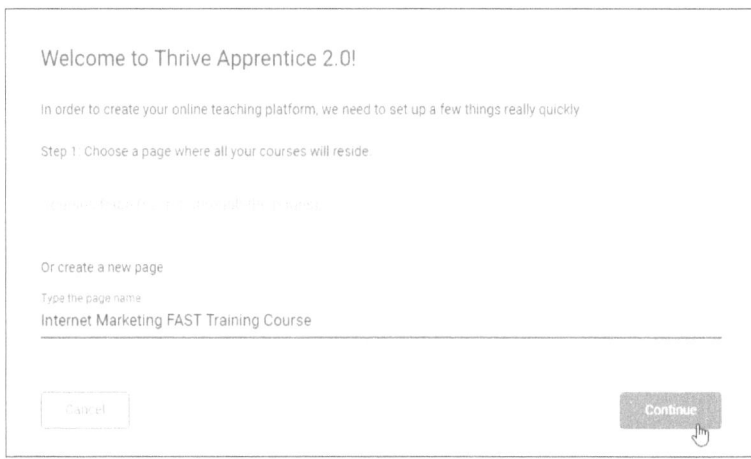

Figure 107: Select or Create Your Training Page

Then click the **Continue** button.

The next step is template setup. You can personalize the template or use the default one.

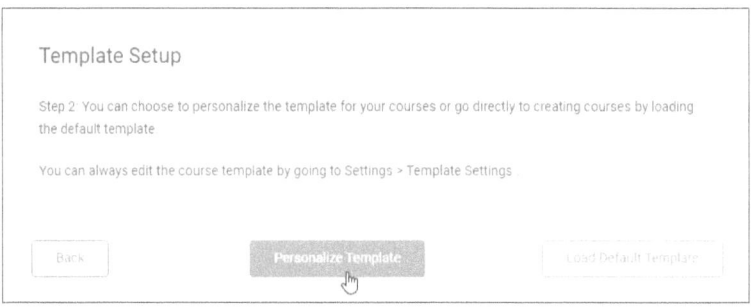

Figure 108: Set up the Course Template

If you choose **Personalize Template**, you can make some simple changes, such as the primary color and logo.

If you choose **Load Default Template**, you are taken directly to the course builder. You can always modify the template later, so this is the best way to get started.

Courses built with Thrive Apprentice have a 3-tier structure.

The top level is Modules, then Chapters then Lessons. That is, Modules contain Chapters, which in turn contain Lessons.

However, this is totally flexible.

For example, you can leave Chapters out and just have a Module containing Lessons. This could be the model for a small course.

Or you could just create lessons until you start to see the groupings that are appropriate. Then create chapters and drag and drop lessons into them.

Thrive Apprentice is very flexible.

Click Add New Course to start building your course.

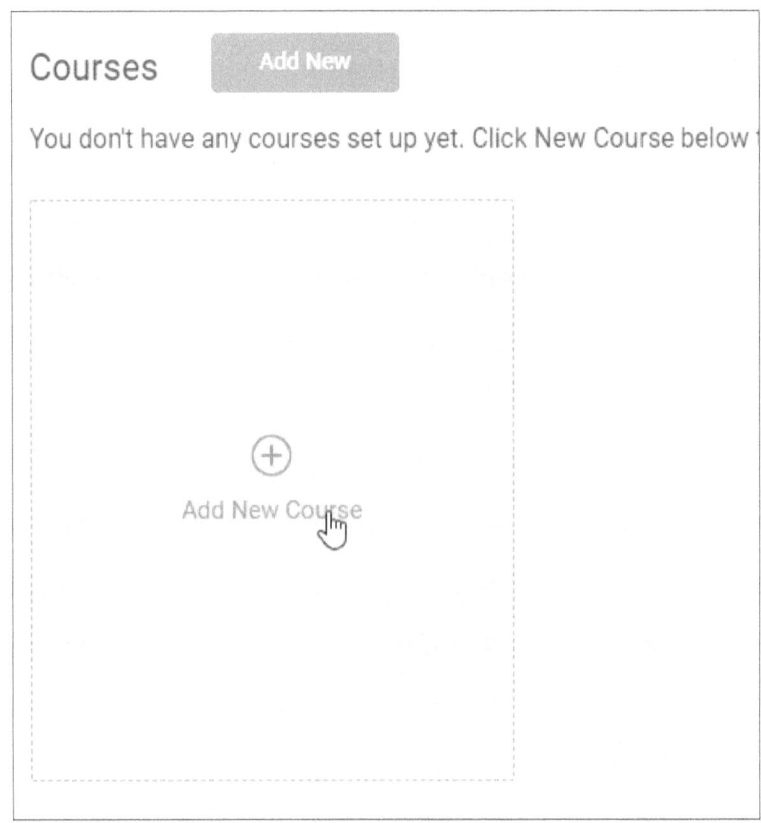

Figure 109: Click Add New Course

Enter a name for your course. Note that by default, it's under a page named Courses. I like this, as you may be building other, related courses later on and this keeps all your courses under the one umbrella.

It also means that any SEO or advertising you do will benefit all courses.

Internet Marketing Fast

Become a Thrive Expert

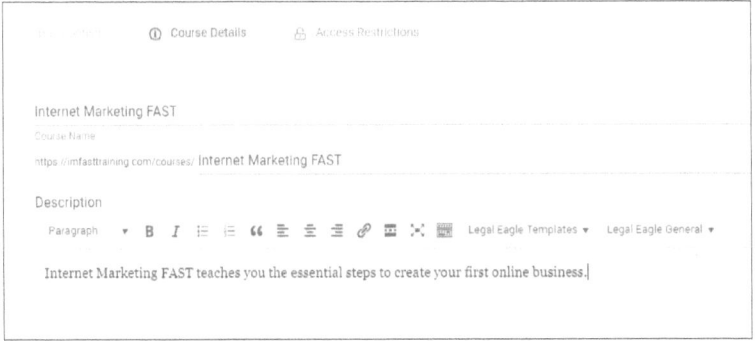

Figure 110: Enter the Course Name and Description

Note that you must enter a description to proceed but don't stress about that as you can always change it later.

Then click the **Save** button.

Return by clicking **Back to Dashboard**.

You will see that your course has been created.

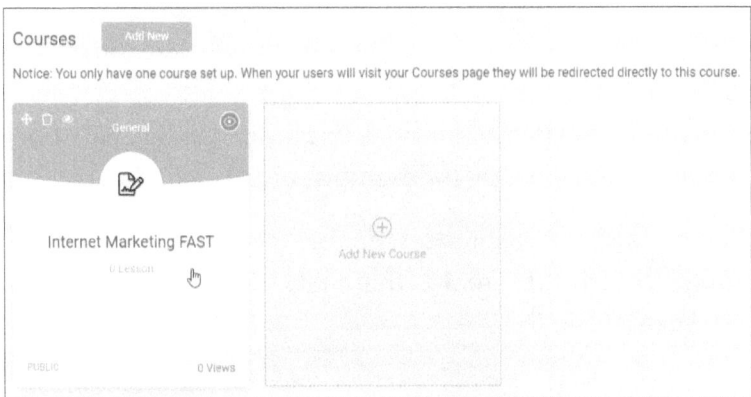

Figure 111: Course Has Been Created

Internet Marketing Fast

Become a Thrive Expert

As this is your first (only) course, you will see a message explaining that when a visitor enters the Courses page, they will go straight to this course.

You should see three tabs:

- Content
- Course Details
- Access Restrictions

Under *Content*, you can click the + sign and start entering Modules, Chapters and Lessons. They can be done in any order.

Under *Course Details*, you can update the description that you entered when creating the course, upload a cover image, add a video description, allow or disallow comments and add some details about you as the teacher.

Under *Access Restrictions*, you decide who has access to your course. By default, everyone does, but you can set it up so that only logged in users, or only customers who have purchased the course, for example, are allowed to access it.

You can also make some lessons exempt from this rule. You could use this to make the first two lessons free for instance.

Internet Marketing Fast

Become a Thrive Expert

Figure 112: Access Restrictions

There's a lot more to ensuring that only buyers of the course have access to it, of course, but that's beyond the scope of this book.

Lessons, Chapters and Modules

You add a lesson, chapter or module by clicking on the corresponding tab.

For a Module, you add the title, description and optionally a cover image. You can also specify whether or not comments are allowed.

For a Chapter, you add just the title.

For a Lesson, you add the title, description and optionally a cover image. You can also specify whether or not comments are allowed.

But you can also define the lesson as text, audio or video. Audio and video lessons can be hosted from a platform such as SoundCloud or YouTube. Or they can be hosted from your website.

For YouTube, a number of other options are available to improve the user experience.

Figure 113: Lesson YouTube Options

You can preview your course at any time but it can't be seen by visitors until you publish it. You must have completed at least one lesson before you can publish a course.

Thrive Comments

Thrive Comments allows you to manage and interact with your audience's comments in ways not available through the standard WordPress interface.

Install it from the Thrive Product Manager.

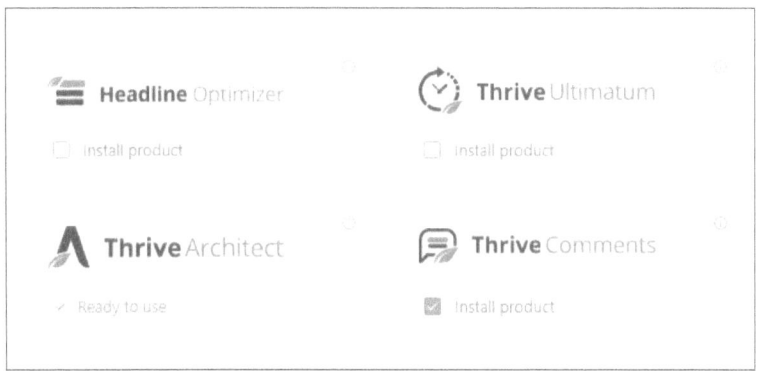

Figure 114: Install Thrive Comments

With Thrive Comments, you can reward your commenters with instant feedback, much like social platforms.

How about redirecting first time commenters to a 'welcome to the community' free gift page? What about showing repeat commenters a social share button so they can post their comment (and your post) to Facebook as well?

With Thrive Comments you can set post-comment actions. Anything from redirecting a commenter to a URL, showing related posts, giving social sharing prompts, or when combined with Thrive Leads, opening a lightbox.

Make commenting frictionless for your audience by allowing visitors to leave a comment straight from their social accounts, no sign in required. Combine this with an after-comment prompt to share the article on social - and the ability to share individual post comments - and you've got yourself a recipe for Social Media success.

Internet Marketing Fast

Become a Thrive Expert

You set up how you want comments handled from the Thrive Comments dashboard.

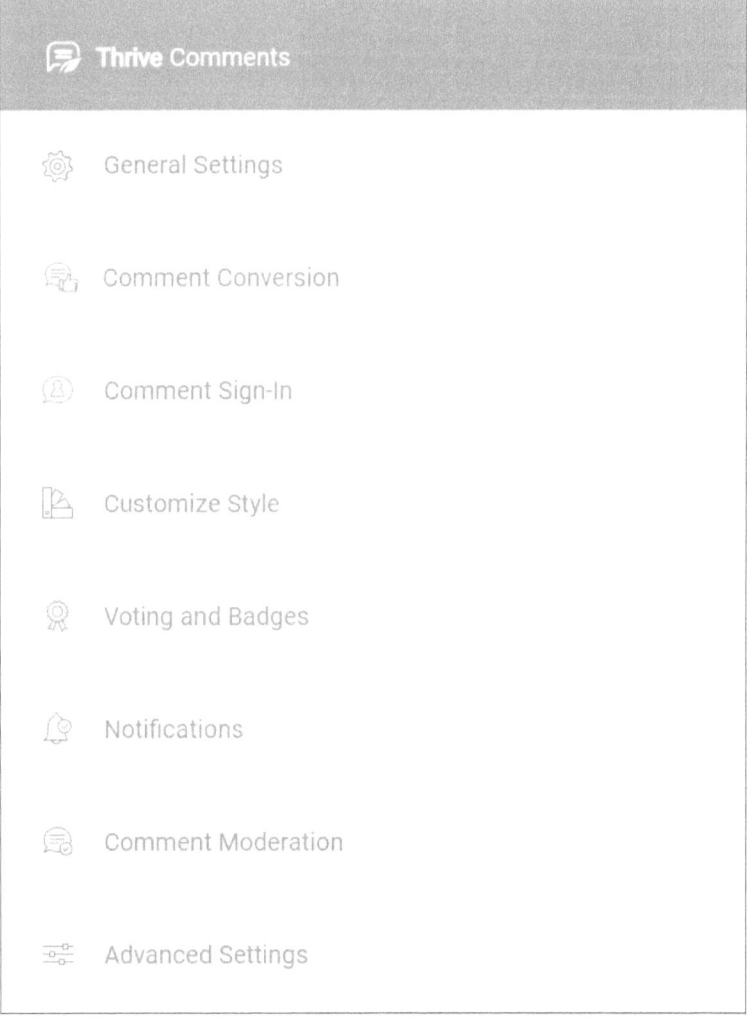

Figure 115: Thrive Comments Dashboard

Internet Marketing Fast

Become a Thrive Expert

Click on the down arrow next to each setting to set it up.
For example, Voting and Badges:

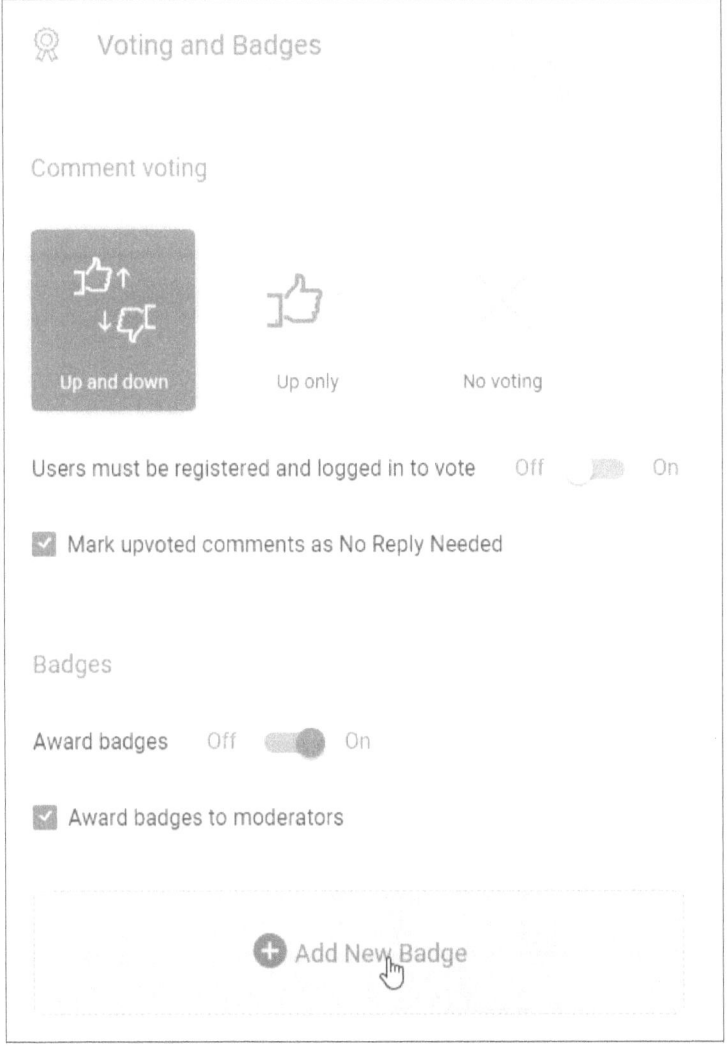

Figure 116: Set up Voting and Badges

Internet Marketing Fast

Thrive Optimize

Thrive Optimize is a simple A/B testing add-on for Thrive Architect that gives you the power to run fast and highly effective split tests for your landing pages - directly on your WordPress website.

Install it from the Thrive Product Manager.

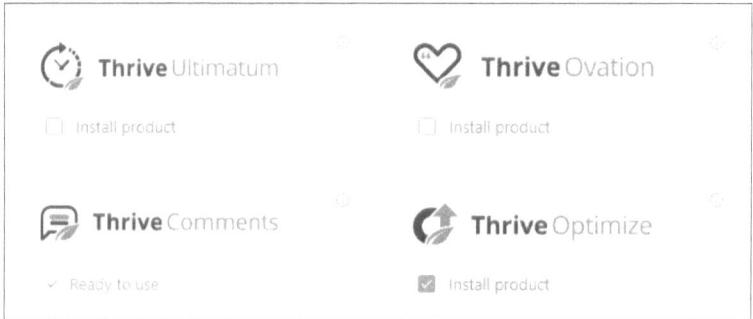

Figure 117: Install Thrive Optimize

Thrive Headline Optimizer split tests different headlines on a page. Thrive Optimize split tests entire landing pages. So for example, you could split test a video opt-in page against a text opt-in page.

Once you've installed Thrive Optimize, load the page you want to split test into Thrive Architect.

Then click on A/B test (a new icon) in Architect's menu.

Internet Marketing Fast

Become a Thrive Expert

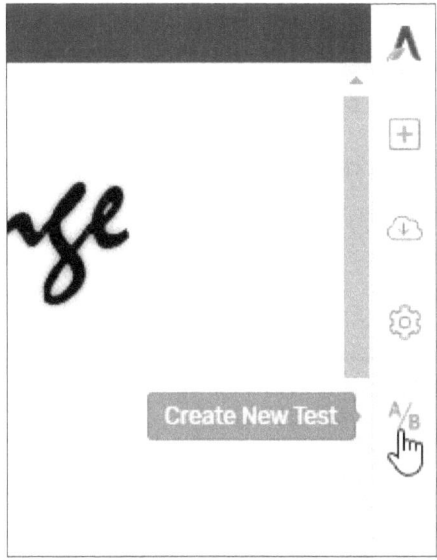

Figure 118: Click on A/B Test

You can then add a new page to be A/B tested against the original one.

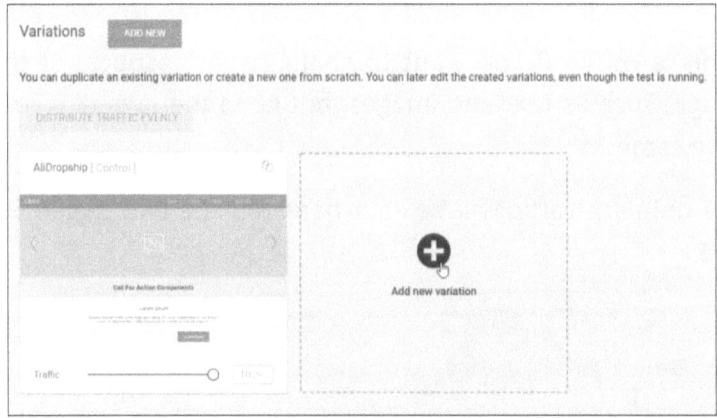

Figure 119: Add the Page Variation

Internet Marketing Fast

Become a Thrive Expert

As soon as you click on the + button, a new empty page will be created and can be edited. This is useful if you want to create an entirely different style of page for the test.

Alternatively, you can duplicate the existing page.

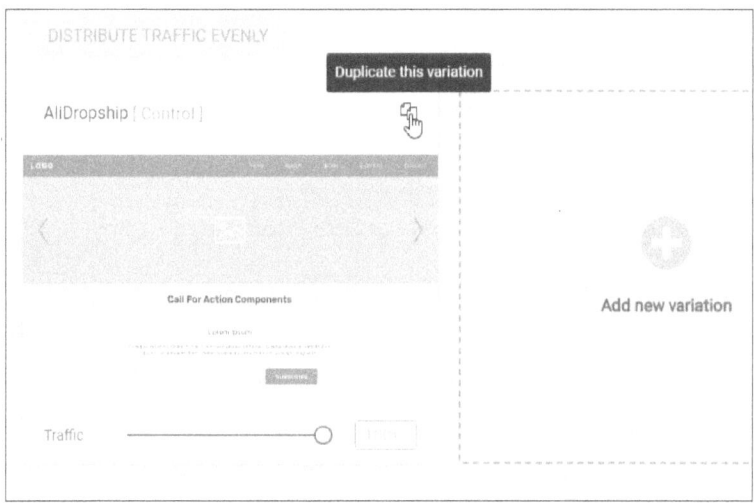

Figure 120: Duplicate Control Page

This is useful if you want to change some aspects of the page, such as text and images, but keep the overall layout the same.

By default, traffic will be split between the two pages 50-50.

Internet Marketing Fast

Become a Thrive Expert

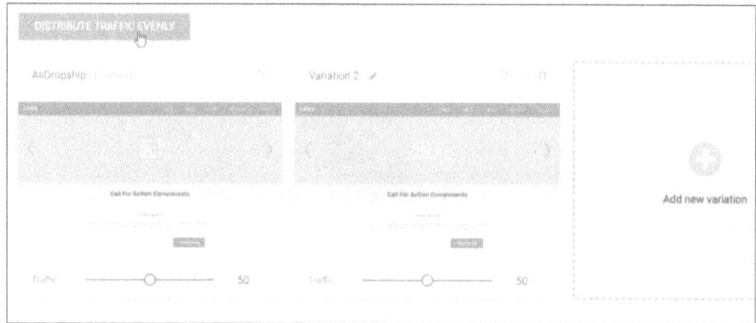

Figure 121: Two Variations Created

You can add more pages if you want, but it's simpler to work with two at a time.

Once you've edited the cloned page to your satisfaction, you can start the A/B test.

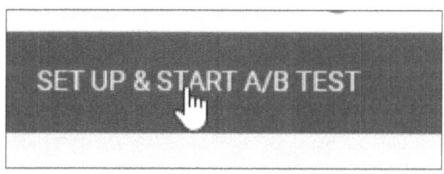

Figure 122: Set up the A/B Test

You need to personalize your test with a name, description, how long it should run and conditions for picking a winner.

Internet Marketing Fast

Become a Thrive Expert

Figure 123: Personalize Your Test

Then set the goal (it can be revenue, visits to another page or subscriptions).

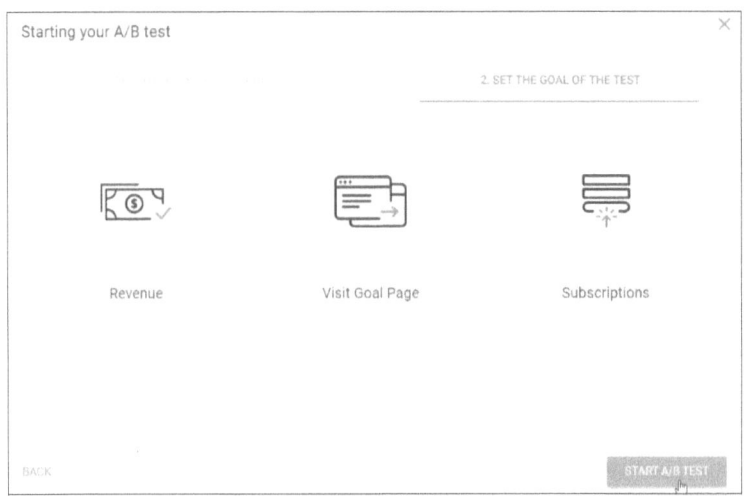

Figure 124: Set the Goal and Start the Test

Internet Marketing Fast

Become a Thrive Expert

Clicking on any of these requires further information. For example, if you select revenue, then you can select (or create) the thank you page that corresponds to a purchase.

Once you've started the A/B test, you can go to the Thrive Optimize dashboard at any time to see the results.

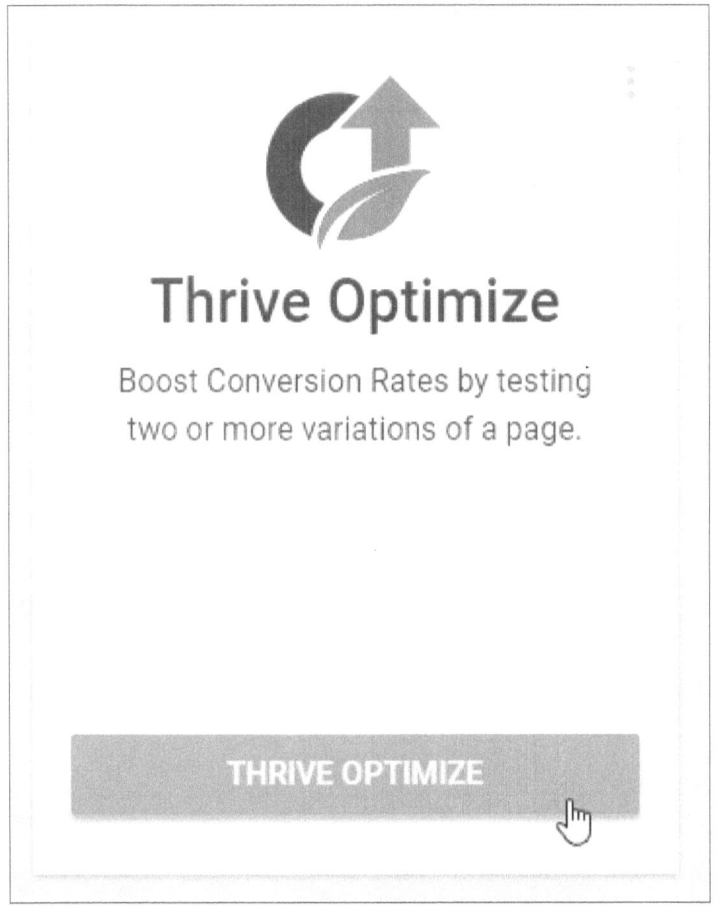

Figure 125: Thrive Optimize Dashboard

Internet Marketing Fast

Become a Thrive Expert

This will show the current results, including the number of visitors, sales etc. depending on which goal was chosen.

Internet Marketing Fast
Become a Thrive Expert

The Rest of the Books

Here are all the books in my Internet Marketing FAST series, all available as Kindle Singles.

Available Now

1. The 4 Things You Must Know (to Make Money While You Sleep)
2. How to Select Your Internet Marketing Niche
3. How to Register a Domain Name
4. How to Host Your Website
5. WordPress for the Technically Challenged
6. Building Your Website with Thrive
7. Continue Your Journey with Thrive
8. Become a Thrive Expert

Not Yet Available

9. Become an Affiliate Marketing Ninja
10. Become an E-Commerce Ninja
11. The Deadly Combo of Blog Posts and Landing Pages
12. Google is Your New Best Friend
13. Building Your Mailing List
14. All About Free and Paid Traffic
15. How to Publish Your Book on Amazon
16. The Secret to Making Money with Your Internet Businesses (after You've Done Everything Else)

Internet Marketing Fast

Become a Thrive Expert

You can get the Kindle and Paperback links to the books on Amazon at

https://superaffiliatechallenge.com/internet-marketing-fast-books-from-amazon/

Internet Marketing Fast

Become a Thrive Expert

About the Author

As an 80 year old (in 2024) fitness fanatic and successful internet marketer, Phil Lancaster is a bit of an anomaly.

Through a combination of bad luck and bad business decisions, he found himself broke and alone at 74.

Now, a few years later, he has several internet businesses that combine to bring him a 6-figure income.

It wasn't easy and he got burned a few times on the way, but he reckons that anyone can do it with the right road map.

He wants to help you to get started the way he did, but without making the same mistakes.

Anyone, from student to baby boomer (and older) can make money through the internet.

Phil's IM Fast series of mini-books will get you started. At just $2.99 each, you won't find a better investment.